TALKING TO MY ANGELS

ALSO BY MELISSA ETHERIDGE

The Truth Is…

TALKING TO MY ANGELS

MELISSA ETHERIDGE

HARPER WAVE

An Imprint of HarperCollins*Publishers*

Some of the names that appear in this book have been changed to protect privacy.

HarperCollins books may be purchased for educational, business, or sales promotional use. For information, please email the Special Markets Department at SPsales@harpercollins.com.

FIRST EDITION

Library of Congress Cataloging-in-Publication Data

Names: Etheridge, Melissa, author.
Title: Talking to my angels / Melissa Etheridge.
Description: First edition. | New York : Harper Wave, 2023. | Identifiers: LCCN 2023022334 (print) | LCCN 2023022335 (ebook) | ISBN 9780063257450 (hardcover) | ISBN 9780063257481 (epub)
Subjects: LCSH: Etheridge, Melissa. | Rock musicians–United States–Biography. | Women rock musicians–United States–Biography. | Lesbian musicians–United States–Biography. | LCGFT: Autobiographies.
Classification: LCC ML420.E88 A3 2023 (print) | LCC ML420.E88 (ebook) | DDC 782.42166/092 [B]--dc23/eng/20230519
LC record available at https://lccn.loc.gov/2023022334
LC ebook record available at https://lccn.loc.gov/2023022335

23 24 25 26 27 LBC 5 4 3 2 1

For my son Beckett who is with me every day in the nonphysical.
I've been talking to my Angel, and he said that it's all right…

CONTENTS

CONTENTS

PART I

BEFORE AND AFTER

CHAPTER 1

YOU MAY KNOW ME

You may know me as a rock star. Ever since I released my first album in 1988, I've been writing songs, touring the world, performing as much as I can—music has been my heartbeat and my path. Like many an artist, creating is my way of processing my experience. Some of my songs emerge straight from my life—the ups and downs of relationships, the confusion and conflicts that I've wrestled with. Some of my songs are reflections on events that have shocked the world—9/11, violence against LGBTQIA+ communities, the issue of climate change affecting our natural world. Creation helps me understand. Creation keeps me asking questions. Creation is what I've needed to keep going.

You may know me from the stories I have shared from my life, in my songs, in my writing, in my advocacy: that I grew up in Kansas, that my mom was distant and cold, that my dad drove me to gigs so I could perform, starting at the ripe old age of eleven. I wrote about some of these things in my first book over twenty years ago. But I've come around to a different kind of understanding in this second part of life.

Something happened that radically changed the way I under-stand myself, the events of my life, and how I fit into the world around me. Many people have described sudden changes in who we are as epiphanies or moments of great insight. For me it was an experience that jump-started a spiritual awaken-ing that has moved me into a wholly new way of living a daily practice that has helped me heal—from old childhood wounds, the disappointments of former relationships, and feelings that I've tried to ignore—anger, shame, and a bad case of self-doubt.

I feel blessed, for this radical shift has widened my understanding of my past and offered me a fresh framework and a more textured context to help me tell a more fulsome account of my life thus far. I am also grateful for the chance to revisit some of these old stories and, more, to share some new ones. I want to invite you into a deeper understanding of the pain and the beauty along the way. Sometimes they are one and the same.

While all of these stories illustrate dimensions of my experience and have given my life shape and meaning, they don't define me. For years I compartmentalized difficult emotions and disguised my real feelings in songs, letting people see only what I thought they wanted from me, what made things easier for them, what would make them love me like I wanted to be loved. Now I know that I am more than these parts—or even the sum of them. I am a messy (and glorious) whole.

Of course, any life has many befores and afters—before I could walk and after I could run. Before I could play the guitar and after I could play the piano. The first time I fell in love and then, after, when I realized that there's not just one person on this earth that I could love beyond measure. But I'm talking about a really big be-fore and a really big after.

It happened one hot summer Saturday night in LA in 2003. I was hanging out with my then-new girlfriend, Tammy. Tammy and I had started what had felt like an easy-breezy thing, with no big intentions at the moment. I just wanted to get a little bit stoned and relax. My kids, Bailey and Beckett, were with their other mother, my former partner, Julie. I was in a good mood. The long-drawn-out breakup with Julie felt like it might finally be ending. I'd bought a cool new house in Mandeville Canyon, and I was ready to put the past behind me. Get on with my life. Be a cool mom for my kids. I wanted only lightness. Fun. A breather.

So on this hot Saturday night, Tammy decided to make chocolate chip cookies—she happened to be a really good baker. Someone had given us some cannabis, so I suggested she add some to the batter—what the heck, right? I didn't actually see how much cannabis she had blended in with the chocolate morsels, but I do remember the heavenly sweet aroma as they began to bake.

We were kicking back, listening to music, and enjoying the cookies. Then I began to feel a shift—not an earthquake. More like a slow inner spin. I began to laugh as the room slowly melted away and I felt keenly present.

The music seemed louder and more intense. The lyrics being sung had greater clarity. My skin felt tingly, and a blanket of warmth moved over me, as I relaxed deeply.

Inside this deep state of relaxation, I was also super stimulated.

I'd enjoyed cannabis before, but this night was different. Something big was happening.

When my good friend and tour manager Steven came by the house for me to sign some papers, I was sitting on the sofa hysterically laughing. Steven saw that there were no kids around, but he also saw that something was up—I was usually not so out of my mind. Probably not a good time for me to sign anything, but I did.

Tammy had pretty much passed out, and I had helped her to bed.

I looked up to find Steven looking down at me, smiling. He took in the scene, and laughed softly. He's one of my best friends and always, always has my back. He made sure I was okay and then he left.

I was alone.

I'm not really a partier—I drank more than usual when I was with Julie, but for many years I barely touched alcohol. Julie and I had gotten into a pattern that I call "auto-drinking"—a habit that was yet another sign that she and I were so distant from each other, the alcohol and partying taking the place of any real love or intimacy. It wasn't hard for me to stop because I hated the way the alcohol made me feel. Hated waking up feeling fuzzy and not in sync with my body.

The night I ate those chocolate chip cookies, I began to trip on a heroic dose of cannabis. A heroic dose is what one calls a significant amount of a substance that can create hallucinogenic effects. And boy, did those cookies pack a punch.

Even though I wasn't moving, I felt like I was on a roller coaster, trying to relax with the ascent and brace myself for sudden drops. Both giddy and afraid, I did not understand what was happening. I figured I was really high—that seemed pretty obvious. But it was a different kind of high—the quality of my attention was more intense. I *was perceiving* into my surroundings, not simply observing. It was a roller coaster of dizzying awareness. I remember the light from the outdoor patio slanting in through the windows, heightening the plush of the carpet. I ran my hands through the textured fabric on the sofa, feeling the sensation on my fingertips and finding it funny. I swear I could hear the texture and taste the color.

I felt both in and outside of my body. I didn't want to move, but I had the sensation of moving and felt an electric energy course through me, pulsing my blood, and quickening my breath. Despite all of this movement within me, I was simultaneously very still.

I had lost all sense of time—was it still night? How long ago was Steven here? Minutes or hours?

My body had lost its boundaries and seemed to have merged with the environment around me. It felt like I was not of my body, not restricted by it.

Then I began to see my thoughts. Images of my life collided before me out of sequence but with vivid clarity: my daughter, Bailey, being born. Performing at my first women's music festival. Being in my bus on tour, tucked into my bed with my guitar, strumming along as the highways passed outside the small window. Beckett's cry when he took his first breath. I could see myself up onstage when I was a little girl, singing my heart out. Sitting beside my dad in his Cutlass Supreme as we crisscrossed Kansas going to gigs, listening to the radio, just the two of us. I could feel the sharp winter air of Boston. I could taste my grandmother Annie Lou's coconut cake, the sweet nirvana on my tongue, the pure pleasure of being in her kitchen.

Time collapsed and these memories were no longer distant but nearer to me, and in the flow of them, it felt like all of me was coming back to myself, as if I'd been lost before but didn't know it. I felt incredibly alive.

I also heard voices talking to each other about me, and I was overhearing their conversation.

"Should we tell her?"

"Tell her what?"

"Well, the meaning of life."

I then received a kind of download of information and the arrival of a new understanding.

And that understanding?

That everything is made of love—even the most horrible thing is made of love. War, death, sickness—all of life is contained within a capsule of love. I didn't quite know what to make of this. How could horrible things and great difficulties also be made of love? The answer that arose from within was that love was what was left after all—after the good and the bad, we are left with love.

I thought of my music and how when I begin to create, I am pulled along like on a river current sometimes rushing downstream, other times gliding lazily with a surprising eddy spinning me sideways. Either way, I am one with the water and let myself be carried. I hear the emergence of a song in my head, I see how the story behind lyrics or the music itself comes forth from some inner place. With music, I know that I am trying to express certain feelings or capture their meaning in the song, but it's not an intellectual exercise; it's giving into that current of energy and letting it take me wherever it's going. It's an experience of surrender, which does not come easily to me except in the creation of music.

This is how I let creation happen. I don't force anything. I trust that it will take shape and make sense.

Now, at the height of this trip, I was seeing into my own creative process, understanding that I had always had the capacity for this other kind of knowing but now I was aware of it.

All this was happening as I lay still on the sofa, plugged into all these thoughts and feelings swirling around me. I tried to follow the thread: if music was how I experience creation, and the essence of creation was love, wasn't I capable of creating love? Were they one and the same?

I became suffused with love, giving in to the space around my body and merging into an infinite horizon. By whom was I loved? And who was generating this love? Was it possible to imagine being loved? And in that imagining, make it real?

As these questions arose in a burst of spontaneous and tangible insight, I began to realize that it was me doing the loving. That for the first time ever, I felt a profound self-love.

And I shattered into tears.

The universe was trying to tell me that I did not have to be afraid. That I did not have to worry. That I did not have to fight so hard for what I wanted. That the love moving through me, the love that runs through all of us and connects us to one another, to the sky and trees, the animals and plants—the all of it—that the love is within us and all around us. If love is the biggest constant, then might we be able to guide ourselves—our decisions, our thoughts, and our feelings—our very way of being in the world? It seemed very simple to me: every choice is a choice between love or fear. The question is: Can we love in the face of fear? It's a both/and, not an either/or, proposition. There was a lot to learn.

I was receiving a kind of download in bits and pieces, none of it quite making sense intellectually but all of it making sense on some other kind of frequency that I was just beginning to embody. I felt strongly that I was on the edge of something, though at the time, I didn't quite have the words for it. But I can say this with absolute clarity: this experience moved me into a different state of mind and a new way to live. And though it didn't happen in one fell swoop, this heroic dose of cannabis catapulted me forward onto a path of spiritual awakening.

Believe me, I never imagined evolving into this person. If you'd told me at the beginning of my career that I'd become a spiritual being having a human experience, I would have dismissed it as nonsense, despite my having always thought of myself as being spiritually minded. This was a whole other level. Thirty years ago, I was living life at full speed. I was riding my fame and music career like a dirt bike at high speed, taking all the bumps, the hills, the narrow trails, looking only forward as I carved my dreams into reality, worked my ass off, and made a name for myself. You see, I liked this image of me: soft on the outside but tough as nails on the inside. But that wasn't exactly true. I'm much more vulnerable than I have cared to admit.

Sure, I liked the perks of hanging out with other people whose stars were rising—most of the time—but I didn't really care about how their fame may or may not rub off on me. I was in my own lane, playing my music, totally focused on my goal: I wanted fame and glory for my music. I wanted to be a rock star.

I know that sounds audacious. But I have to be honest with myself: that was me at that time and for all those years. When I did become famous, when my songs were at the top of the charts, and I had become a public persona attracting attention and earning the label of "celebrity," I realized pretty quickly that fame answers none of the big questions. In fact, it helps you to hide from them, at least for a while. Ultimately it forces you to seek out different questions.

My relationship to fame has changed over time. I used to want it, crave it, because when I was young, I thought fame guaranteed me love and acceptance, that it was an end goal. But that's a lie anyone pursuing fame tells themselves. Love and acceptance have to come from within before you can accept and honor them from others.

It's taken a while—years in fact—to take what I experienced that night and to put it into practice, a practice for which I am so very grateful. Learning to choose love over fear is what in many ways prepared me to confront, surrender to, and heal from one of the most devastating events of my life: the loss of my second-oldest child, Beckett, who died three months into the pandemic lockdown. Beckett died of an opioid overdose after becoming addicted to drugs, and succumbed when fentanyl shut down his lungs and stopped his heart.

In the months and years before his death, while he suffered from depression and addiction, I questioned my capacity to love. I felt so much guilt, so much sadness, so much pain. Was I doing all I could for Beckett? Was my use of cannabis a factor in his opioid addiction? Should I have cut him loose and stopped paying for rehab, wilderness programs? Should I have refused to support him financially, to somehow give him the signal that I believed he could take care of himself given the chance? Should I have said no more than I said yes? How does one love a child and lose that child? How does one make the unbearable bearable? These questions and doubts plagued me, kept me up at night, and nearly drove me crazy while I tried to figure out how best to help him. When he died, these questions haunted me still but with the brutal clarity that none of my ruminations would bring him back.

But this book is not about Beckett's death. It's about how I somehow came to accept it and kept on living afterward—for my children, my wife, and myself. The pain will never leave me, and yet, still, I am alive and well. I still not only believe in love, I choose love each and every day. I experience joy, and I continue to create. My music has always been my balm and my salve, something I've relied on in my darkest moments. I have realized that moving forward, believing in hope, and accepting myself and all the other contradictions in this world is the only way through. The only option to despair.

Love is where I live now. Love is my vibe. It's my channel. It may sound corny or too woo-woo—I get it. But I have to speak and write from this place, because it's the most real for me. I hope you come to see what I mean in these pages.

This new way of being in love is what grounds me. And though it was an accidental ingestion of an enormous amount of cannabis that catapulted me into another level of consciousness, perhaps I was going there anyway. I am now certain that love makes every-thing possible: it's led me to my relationship with Spirit and my relationship with my wife, Linda. My love for my children helped me to get there as well, as it's a kind of love that continues to sur-prise me in its vulnerability. What do these experiences all share? They are reminders to me that I am LOVE.

There are many ways to experience and get in touch with this vibe. At one level, it's quite simple: I try to remain open and aware and to listen for what I already know. Sometimes I need a vehicle, like music. For others it can be as simple as tending a garden, reading a book, or loving another person; some find it through religion, rituals, a relationship with God. We are not here to judge anyone's path, but to simply bear witness to one another's journeys.

What does living with Spirit entail?

For me, it's a daily practice that has emerged from a period of spir-itual awakening when I became newly aware of and connected to the vast unseen dimension where my soul resides. Living in Spirit is also a practice of gratitude, a conscious nurturing of faith in the essential goodness of people, and an awareness that fears are information to pay attention to. Reaching an understanding of how to live this way did not happen overnight but evolved through a continued pondering of how I could live a meaningful life as an expression of love. I didn't want to just say I chose love, I wanted to live it.

So living in Spirit is a daily practice in which I:

- Choose love over fear
- Foster creativity because it's the source of our ability to adapt and move on
- Treat all with kindness and compassion
- Am authentic and honest with myself and others
- Embrace what comes into my life
- Appreciate the lessons and opportunities to grow
- Resist controlling others or outcomes
- Surrender to pain when it inevitably comes
- Trust the healing energy of the universe
- Honor the connection with fellow humans, animals, and plants
- Accept that joy and sorrow coexist—they don't cancel each other out

It is my hope that over the next pages you see how I arrived at this way of loving and living.

The bottom line is that I have love and I lean into that love every moment I can. It feeds me, fuels me, awakens me. Each morning I wake up and ask myself, *Okay, how can I serve love today? How can I lead with love?* Some days it's easier to answer those questions than others.

On the days when it's harder, when I wake up and think about Beckett and miss him so badly that my chest hurts, I breathe. I sink into the discomfort and try my best to not avoid it. I breathe and remind myself that love is a powerful protection but it comes with a price: I would not miss Beckett with a profundity that threatens to break me unless I kept my heart open to my love for him. My love for my son and the physical loss of him cannot be separated; I can't run away from either. This truth comes with the necessity of being fully honest with oneself at all times. It can hurt. The alternative is to shut your heart down, and that is not living in truth or love.

*   *   *

Today, as I write these words, I am home, taking care of my kids while I'm not on tour; I'm in between shows, working on various projects. It's early morning, and I sit in my favorite chair in the sunny part of my bedroom. I stop writing and begin to strum one of my first guitars—a Stella—and I think about a new song that is coming to consciousness. This is often how my songs begin. I wake early, grateful for the quiet, bucolic area north of the LA sprawl where I live. I bought this house early in my relationship with my now-ex, Tammy, after we learned she was pregnant with our twins Johnnie Rose and Miller. The house is made for kids: its big, airy rooms, its toys, games, the sprawling kitchen with skateboard marks on the floor—all loving reflections of raising four active kids.

After a breakfast of oatmeal and honey, Linda goes off to do her thing, and I move into the center of the house, an extension of the foyer. This is my reading library and also where I sit at my puzzle table, stacks of boxes proof of my obsession. I face outward toward the backyard with its giant trees and tinkling bird feeders and succulent plants that I tend when I'm home. The front door is to my back, as is the staircase. I sit at my puzzle table to begin my day. This is a thinking spot for me. I often "work" from this position, so I can hear the comings and goings of the kids. I'm not an overlord—not my style. But they are at ages where a little oversight goes a long way.

I look around at my sun-filled house, the photos adorning its walls an homage to my children and how they've changed over time. I catch a glimpse of young Beckett, framed in a black-and-white photo, and I smile.

I am now in a different place as a parent to shepherd the lives of my children the best I can. I'm in a different place with myself, too, and I want to share the story of both my spiritual awakening and how it ultimately helped me recover from the loss of my child. So please know that this is not a story about death. It's really about the mighty power of Spirit, because it was Spirit that came calling for me. It's about how Linda showed me what love really means.

Ultimately this book is an ode to love. It's a testament to vanquishing fear and learning to embrace all of what life brings us, an unvarnished reflection on the many threads of my life.

CHAPTER 2

MADE FOR MUSIC

As you may have guessed, there must have been a lot of cannabis in the chocolate chip cookies, which is why I refer to the whole of that event as my "heroic dose"–shorthand for an experience that some people call a "trip" and others call a "journey." I think of that night and where it took me as a mind-blowing mental, emotional, and spiritual explosion that cleared the way for me to see and understand a fuller reality, and it absolutely and completely changed me forever.

In the days and weeks that followed, I was confused and disoriented. I knew something had happened to me, but I wasn't quite sure what. I also didn't understand what it all meant. I didn't want to talk about it. I wanted to just keep the awareness of it to myself, wanted everything I felt that night to stay real and present, so that I could continue to bask in this visceral, sensual knowing. I sensed that I had a new, raw awareness of myself and my surroundings. Every cell of my being seemed to be wired with energy. I just didn't know what to do with it all.

But almost immediately I was confronted with an enormous problem: I was now a different person than I was before. I could no longer deny that my life before had been incomplete, that something was missing in a major way.

I began thinking about how for most of my life, I'd been a compartmentalizer, separating good from bad—feelings, experiences, friends, lovers, even guitars—putting them into neat little boxes in my mind, fearing, I guess, that if one touched the other then the good would get tarnished or dwindle, and the bad would grow or metastasize.

Things I liked about myself were neatly arranged in the front of the drawer, and what I didn't like, I'd hide deep in the back. I did the same with feelings—I'd face the world with humor, inviting conversations, making people laugh, enthusiastically sharing my energy to make others feel good. But the troubling, anxious, doubt-filled, and uncomfortable feelings? They didn't see the light of day. Maybe they wound their way into a song, but even then, the lyrics would not be about me. I'd have created a story about someone else and kept myself from view. Without being aware, I hid in my music, in relationships, in my nonstop compulsion to work. I saw now that I'd been living this way for years, separating my feelings, showing only a partial view of myself to the world, while I pushed the other parts deep into shadow, where they lay tied to shame, self-doubt, fear—negative emotions that seemed too big for me to handle or admit to.

I now sensed that this habit of compartmentalizing was actually making sure I stayed attached to things that caused me pain. I didn't really get that, in trying so hard to hide my vulnerabilities, I was just making myself more vulnerable.

I had done this for as long as I could remember, a way of forcing myself to be strong, reliable, and forthright. Now, I felt exposed, and I was getting a very clear message that it was no longer possible for me to live a life where I did any kind of hiding from the truth of myself as a whole. The sheer breadth of the experience had blown me open, the force of which having jettisoned all the negative thoughts and feelings stuffed in the dresser drawers on the floor in a giant pile that I now wanted—needed—to sort through.

Now, exquisitely (and necessarily, uncomfortably) vulnerable, I felt compelled to get really naked with myself, so in the days, weeks, and months after the heroic dose, I returned to my first story about myself in an effort to uncover the hidden truths that I now needed to bring into the light.

*   *   *

My mom told me my birth story, how at almost forty weeks pregnant, her water broke and she was having contractions, but the nurses at the local hospital closed her legs to stop labor. She was ready to deliver. I was ready to be born. The doctor, however, was apparently not ready—or present. He was on his lunch or dinner break, and the hospital staff told my mother that she had to wait until he returned.

When I was finally delivered, I was black and blue and I had a huge hematoma on my chest, which finally disappeared when I was twenty-one. I'd always thought of the stain as an ugly birthmark, something that made me different.

I was born on May 29, 1961, a day that also fell on my older sister Jenny's birthday. Instead of getting to celebrate her fourth birthday party, she got me: a present, I'd come to learn, she was none too pleased to receive.

I learned all of these details in my thirties, when I did a past-life regression, and the medium picked up on some turbulence. Curious to understand more about what the medium had seen about my entry into the world during this lifetime, I called my mother, who, in her flat, emotionless way, recounted my birth story as if it had happened to someone else. This was a classic response for my mother: little affect, no connection to the trauma of my birth, an implicit request to not ask any more questions. The only detail she offered was a dispassionate reference to my sister being out of sorts because I had arrived on her birthday.

This story seems almost odd to me. There was a lot my mother didn't explain. How could my mother not have shared this? Why was she so emotionless about it?

My mother was a smart, well-educated woman who'd had her own dreams, but by the time she became a mother, she'd essentially given up on those dreams. She was a computer programmer and wrote code for the military at Fort Leavenworth, way before writing code was acknowledged as a lucrative field. Mom often complained that she wasn't paid for all the work she did, meaning that the men—her bosses—took the credit for her work developing war games and other scenarios on computers that took up whole rooms. It's a frustrating old story, a pain point for generations of accomplished women who never got credit for their work.

My mom was also our family's main breadwinner. My dad taught American Government and was the basketball coach at our local high school. He was well regarded at the school and in Leavenworth in general, though he didn't make much money on a public school salary. We lived in a nice, well-appointed house in a clean, middle-class neighborhood in an area within a five-mile radius of four different prisons—the military prison, the federal prison, the men's penitentiary, and the women's penitentiary. That's right, the biggest industry in my hometown was prisons—no wonder I always wanted to escape.

Our house looked like a lot of the houses in our neighborhood—a tight three-bedroom with a small eat-in kitchen, a living room with a fireplace, a television, and later a piano. The neighborhood was safe, despite the nearby inmates, and all the kids in the neighborhood ran through one another's backyards and pedaled road bikes up and down the paved streets. I'm not sure if my parents had envisioned such a suburban life or if they chose it because it was near where my dad had gotten his job teaching.

Although I never wanted for anything, I was always attuned to a low-level of stress about money. My parents didn't talk about it out loud, but I was sensitive to their remarks about the price of gas and groceries, how we could only go to my grandparents in Arkansas for summer vacations, and how "this Christmas is going to be simple." I remember one Christmas when my dad had given my mother a set of three tea towels, wrapping each of them individually.

I was also very aware that my mom controlled the purse strings, even though my dad was the one who shopped for groceries and bought us presents. Later I'd find out through my sister that my mom made twice as much as my dad. She also took care of all the bills and was the accountant for our home. It was understood that she could have made a lot more money if she were a man, and this caused an unspoken but very real tension and accounted for the struggle with money even in a dual-income household. I think that part of her resented working for so little.

I want to believe that my mother married for love, loved my

father and he her, though I never saw them hold hands or kiss. I don't remember them smiling at each other. I didn't feel any warm feelings transmitted. Of course, I was a child and didn't know what I was looking for between them, but even as I grew up there was no evidence of their love, and the tensions in our home were palpable.

When I was young, I blamed the coldness of their relationship on my mom. My dad was the nice guy, the fun parent. He was the one who bought the records that we enjoyed and took me to the movies. My mom rarely accompanied us. She took us to the library and to the dentist or pediatrician.

She was rigid in the way she lived her life. After work, she came home and begrudgingly made dinner. After we all ate in relative silence, she then retreated to the living room with her book, a drink, and small plate of Camembert cheese and crackers. Other times, she went upstairs to her room.

Most nights my dad disappeared into the garage to work on the car or went to the basement to listen to his records. Jenny went out almost every night, even when she was grounded, and I just tried to find a place out of the way to do my homework or listen to the radio. By the time I was ten or eleven years old, I had stopped reading books–something that I had always enjoyed–because books reminded me of my mother, and I was very much determined to do everything in my power to not be like my mother.

One night, when I was in my room, I could hear her crying in her bedroom. I sat on my bed, not sure of what to do. Jenny was out, and my dad must have been in the basement or in the garage. I knew my mother was alone in her room. I rustled up the courage to knock on her door and see if I could do anything to stop those tears.

She lay on the edge of her bed in a fetal position.

"Mom, are you okay? Can I get you anything?"

But she said nothing and continued to cry, weeping audibly and uncontrollably in a low moan. I felt helpless and worried for her and afraid I'd be scolded if I persisted in my questions, so I stuffed those feelings deep inside of me and went to my room.

As I grew up, what became clear was my mother's lack of enthusiasm for her life. She didn't seem to want anything more than to go through the motions of work, to come home, get dinner on the table (with a sigh and very little eye contact), and then get lost inside one of many classics, books that transported her out of her life. When I pull from my memories, I see my mother sitting in her favorite living room chair, angled down toward her book, a glass of something at her side. The tableau carries with it an untouchable aloneness, an image bringing into high relief the signal, radiating off of her, telling me she didn't want to be approached or interrupted.

My relationship with my mom was, like her, distant. When I brought friends home, they would politely wave and say, "Hi, Mrs. Etheridge," but since my mother never looked up, my friends would quickly swallow their greeting or their question and move on.

The few times she seemed interested in me, or I'd ask her directly what she thought of my music, she hesitated, her comments always laced with fear. Once I began to sing, write songs, and play the guitar and piano, I remember her saying, "Don't get your hopes up, Missy."

When I was about ten, I wrote a one-act play and showed it to her. I desperately wanted to impress her since she loved words. She read it quickly and then glanced up and, giving me a tight smile, said, "Oh, honey, that's never going to happen."

By fourteen, when I was teaching myself how to play piano by ear, I began writing the music to accompany lyrics. One time, as she passed through the living room, she said, "Missy, you're just making things up."

Judgment and embarrassment seared through me. My efforts for her approval and validation fell flat. I know now that I was both hurt and concerned for her and those conflicting feelings would surface in my later relationships. When I later got a keyboard, I brought it down to the basement, where she couldn't hear me play.

I always felt that my mother wanted me to be more intellectual, like her. At the start of high school, she wanted me to take a science elective—outdoor botany, which I had zero interest in. On the first day in the outdoor classroom, I fell and sliced my knee. I got out of the class, much to my mother's dismay, but once again I believed I had disappointed her.

I craved her attention, though I was ever fearful of her outright rejection. I would come to learn that my later patterns of chasing women just out of reach and falling for women who were otherwise attached were old patterns for me, rooted in my unrequited love for my own mother.

I see clearly now how unhappy my mother was, though I still don't know where that unhappiness came from. In the absence of understanding, I began to believe that she had given up on herself, abdicating her deeper desires. I often wonder if she had been born in a different era with more opportunity and encouragement, she could have built on her intelligence and education and created a more fulfilling life for herself. Maybe she would have chosen not to be a wife or mother. Clearly women who were born in the 1930s, raised in the '40s, and came of age in the 1950s were not given many options to figure out who they wanted to be or what kind of life they wanted to lead. The limited expectations of the gender roles meant that for women, being a wife and mother was paramount. Sure, there were trailblazers in her generation, but that was a big boulder to push up a hill. And after doing her job outside the house, serving the household, and raising two daughters, she must not have had the strength for it. My mother, like millions of her peers, simply accepted that destiny as her lot in life, perhaps even her responsibility.

I used to carry the weight of my mother's unhappiness inside of me, believing at some level that loving her meant just trying to be better than I was. I didn't know how to make this happen—how I could create another version of myself that might bring a smile to her face. I unwittingly absorbed her pain and made it my own as I tried and failed to meet her implicit expectations, taking on her fears that she wrapped into criticisms and judgments of me.

Later, when I was in my early thirties and living in LA, and my career picked up speed, she and I had one of very few substantive conversations. It was after my dad had died and my mom, who had finally stopped working, seemed to be actually enjoying her retirement in a house I had bought her in sunny Arizona. I called to check in on her, and she recounted a time when I was about twelve and my sister was sixteen. We had taken a family vacation to Colorado, an exceptional luxury for us.

I remembered the trip because I had paid for it with the money I had saved from all my gigs; she remembered the trip for another reason.

"Do you remember, we went on a hike that one day?"

"Yes, Mom, I do. It was blazing hot on that trail," I said delicately, unsure where she was going with the story.

"You and Jenny kept going on ahead. No one cared about me."

Wasn't I the child?

Maybe that was it: I never felt like her child, someone she wanted to take care of. Maybe she expected us to take care of her, but we weren't equipped to do that. I can see the cycle of pain created by needs not being met in any direction. I feel more compassion for her now, after participating in my own complicated family dynamics.

*   *   *

One thing that was clear to me even then was that having to deal with my sister put a lot of pressure on my parents.

"Please behave, I have to deal with your sister." I knew what my mom meant: she needed me to be the good daughter, because Jenny was not at all good. Jenny defied all rules and snuck out. She was sneaking out of the house at night by age twelve. She hung around with older guys who were already out of high school and smoked and drank beer. And though Jenny was smart and pretty—so quick-tongued that I often felt stupid—she took up any energy my mom seemed to have to spare.

From as far back as I can remember, Jenny wreaked havoc for our entire family. She had sudden mood shifts and seemed unable to control her behaviors. One minute the house was calm and the next she would have thrown a rage-filled temper tantrum, sending my father into a tailspin, trying to quiet her. When Jenny was a child, this meant trying to distract her with ice cream or a television show or a ride in his car with the windows down. Later, it was a guitar, a new outfit, her own car. Nothing ever satisfied what she was looking for, and my parents seemed to have no clear idea of what to do. Back then, the option of visiting a doctor or therapist for help was not considered. I think my parents were ashamed that they couldn't control Jenny or her outbursts.

The older she got, the more trouble she got into. She was suspended numerous times for smoking behind the bleachers or for cutting classes. She was brazen and unafraid of any consequences. If my parents grounded her, she went out anyway. If they took away her car, she rode her bike or got picked up by a friend.

Jenny's behavior added to the sense that our family was an emotional tinderbox, ready to go up in flames if any of the rest of us spoke up. I could see the anger on my parents' faces, but they never really yelled at Jenny. My mom would turn away and leave my dad to deal with her. I can still hear my dad trying to reason with Jenny, in his patient, caring way, trying to talk sense into her. His efforts had little effect.

Jenny was unapologetically mean, taking out her ever-brewing storm of feelings on me. She pinched me; she poked me; she hit me. She jumped out of closets to terrify me. I remember the two of us being in the basement, where she held me down on the floor and force-fed me a can of Coke until my eyes burned and I threw up. She knew I hated carbonated drinks.

But there was another level to the misery that Jenny caused. She had also been sexually abusing me since I was six or seven years old. When we were alone—in the basement playing or in the room we shared when we visited my grandparents in Arkansas, she would touch me sexually and demand that I touch her. I was so afraid that if I didn't obey her, she would inflict pain—pull my hair, squeeze my nipple, or cover my mouth with her hand so I couldn't breathe.

I didn't really understand what was going on, but I do remember a gnawing sense that what she was doing and what she was having me do was not right.

I did not breathe a word of this to my parents. There was something so sinister about the touching that I was silenced by a fear I couldn't articulate. I was a little girl. I was being violated by someone older and bigger and more powerful than me. I was terrorized by her and unprotected by my parents. As with many victims of abuse, I felt somehow responsible and shamed by it.

Since I could not predict when my sister would violate me, I never wanted to be home alone with her and often felt unsafe in my own house. She was always lurking, ready to inflict her torture.

As a child, I told myself fantastical stories in an effort to make sense of why Jenny was so cruel and violent. I would imagine that before I was born, she'd been in a terrible accident, lost consciousness, and almost died. Or maybe she had been poisoned? Maybe she was inhabited by an evil spirit? I was clearly letting my imagination get the best of me because I didn't have the capacity to understand, and I had no one to go to for help. Because of Jenny's explosiveness, I got the implicit message that my parents expected me not to cause any problems, not to get upset or complain. I remember times when Jenny was acting out and causing chaos, and my parents seemed to focus on me, scolding me for what I considered the slightest infraction—leaving the lights on when I left a room, not putting away my clothes and leaving my room messy.

But I have to admit that I enjoyed being considered the good one. I got good grades, didn't get in any trouble, and tried my best to ask for as little as possible. I was easygoing, smiled often, and was well-liked by both peers and adults. But the older I got, I used a lot of psychic energy to appear easygoing when inside I was feeling a hot mess, unable to talk about how Jenny hurt me and how scared I was of my own sister. In secret, I cried and scribbled stories and songs in my notebook. I lost myself in TV shows and movies. I was always looking for a way out of feeling so alone and fearful. And because I couldn't figure out a way to tell my parents what Jenny was doing to me, I tried to ignore what was happening, leaving me with a great discomfort and confusion. I was training myself to do what would become a habit of mine: burying these dark moments of pain and shame, hoping they would not escape and cause more damage.

*　　*　　*

Though my mother and sister were dark clouds over my younger years, two forces of love provided a counterbalancing energy, an offering of kindness and fuel for courage. One was the steady love between me and my father and the attention and efforts he made to truly see me. The other was my passion and nascent talent for music. The two are forever entwined, and I will always associate my early love of music with my dad.

I remember listening to his little transistor radio, which he'd place on top of the car parked in the driveway while he was doing odd chores around the house. As he whistled or sang to the music, he smiled, which is why I started listening and paying attention. Music could make someone happy! When a song came on that I liked, I'd sneak up, stand on my tiptoes, and reach with my six-year-old's arms to turn up the volume. Standing there, focused on the music on the radio, I tapped my feet and moved to the rhythms of the music. I listened to music every moment that I could. On television, on the radio, playing records. Music surrounded me, and even when not in proximity to its sounds, I heard it in my head and felt it in my body.

My father's taste was eclectic—he liked most of the pop and country they played on WHB Kansas City, the local AM radio station, but his record collection, which he housed in the basement of our house, had a wide range—Broadway shows, Barbra Streisand, Simon & Garfunkel, Neil Diamond, the Mamas & the Papas, Bob Dylan, Aretha Franklin, and a band called CSN whose album cover pictured three hippies sitting on a porch couch. I loved all of it!

Following in my dad's footsteps, I was drawn to varied genres of music. I liked almost everything I heard—country, rock, jazz, show tunes. It was all language of another kind to me, and it all made sense. Nothing was off-limits. It made me open and flexible—and I'm still that way today. Finding my own sound would come later, but my dad's listening habits became my auditory playground.

Then one day it happened! When I was about eight, my father brought home a 1969 Stella by Harmony acoustic six-string guitar.

He walked through the front door and my eyes nearly popped out of my head. I immediately thought the guitar was for me, since he and I had been spending so much time listening to music and no doubt he had seen me strumming the badminton racquet like a lunatic.

He was smiling and looking from my mom to my sister, who were sitting, unusually so, next to each other on the living room couch.

I was on the floor doing a puzzle.

"Here you go," he said, and I watched him hand the guitar to my sister.

I was shocked, heartbroken, and furious! This bright, beautiful guitar was for Jenny? Again, I felt a deep-seated frustration—saw my parents always bending over backward for her.

Jenny looked at me with a glint of satisfaction in her eye. She took the guitar from my dad, strummed its strings a few times, and then glowered at it and just handed it back to my dad.

I started begging my dad, "Please, can I use it? Can it be mine if Jenny doesn't want it?"

"Well, you're going to need lessons," he said in response.

And that's how it all got started. I was eight years old and happily took ownership of that sweet little Stella. My dad went down to Tarbot's Tune Shop, the local record store to inquire about lessons for me. Mr. Don Raymond, who worked at Tarbot's, told my father that I was too young for guitar lessons.

When my dad came home with this news, I only became more resolute: I needed guitar lessons! I don't care if my fingers bleed!

At first, my parents ignored my pleas, but when I persevered, they relented.

So my dad and I went down to Tarbot's Tune Shop (later just the Tune Shop) to talk to Mr. Raymond.

Dark-haired and grumpy, Mr. Raymond took one look at me and said to my father, "She's too young. Her fingers will bleed."

"I don't care," I piped up. "I want to learn how to play. Can you teach me?"

Probably because I looked like I wasn't going to leave the shop without a "yes," Mr. Raymond said (again speaking to my dad, not to me), "She can come in for one lesson, though I'm sure she'll quit because I guarantee her fingers will bleed."

Well, I took that lesson, and my fingers did bleed. But I kept coming back for more. I was in heaven. To this day, I remember the first song I ever played on that guitar—"Twinkle, Twinkle Little Star." Aah, the memories.

For the next two years, I took guitar lessons from Mr. Raymond. I learned that he was a former big-band guitar player who had lost most of the fingers on his left hand in a fiberglass factory accident. He was such a talented musician, he'd taught himself how to play and fret with his right hand, so he could use his left to strum.

I was a bit scared of him—Mr. Raymond wasn't a guy who seemed to like kids. But my desire to learn was bigger than my fear of him. My lessons took place upstairs in the back of the store in a small, dark, and dreary room. But I didn't care—I was on a mission.

I worked with him once a week, and in between, I practiced by myself as much as possible. Mr. Raymond taught me to take my music seriously and how to play notes and chords on the guitar. Later, he would teach me to play classic guitar pieces and complicated jazz combinations, but first I had to master three chords: A, D, and E.

I found in Mr. Raymond someone who loved music as much as I did. He taught me to read music and also how to keep time. When I finally learned how to read music as I played, he would tap his foot and we would play jazz duets. He was stern as he pounded his foot and proclaimed . . . "Doesn't matter what notes you play. Just never go out of time." Slowly, unemotionally he taught me every string. Just recently, I talked to his son, who told me that his father was always proud to have taught me how to play guitar, which means so much to me—because he scared me to death as a kid!

When he taught me those three basic chords—A, D, and E—I proceeded to strum day and night, night and day, driving everyone in my family nuts. Nothing was more important to me than music. Once I knew A, D, and E, I heard them everywhere, in all sorts of music—country, rock, Motown. Those three chords were the key.

I can remember getting my first book of songs from the public library my mother used to take me to, and then I began writing songs of my own, listening to the music in my head and trying to capture my thoughts and feelings into words and lyrics. I wrote on table napkins, scraps of paper, in my school notebooks, and on the back of homework.

Some of my happiest childhood memories revolve around music, especially when my dad and I were alone in the basement, sitting cross-legged on the floor, leaning back against the bean bag chairs he'd bought for the basement. I was held rapt with anticipation and excitement about what music he would play next as he changed the records on the record player. Sometimes we didn't even speak. The music became the communication between us.

Dad was not effusive with compliments, but I took in his encouragement and his belief in me by his constant attention to my musical education and his desire to spend time with me. He had an innate musical sense—"Don't sing through your nose," he reminded me often when I first started singing for him. I'm sure that instruction from him led me to using my chest and developing a deep, open voice when I sing.

For a few years we as a family went to the local Methodist church on Sunday mornings, but our attendance felt more like fulfilling a social expectation rather than any truly religious or spiritually motivated commitment. In other words, neither my dad nor my mom was remotely religious, and I don't even know if they believed in God. We never talked about it.

But I loved going to Sunday school because all the kids in Leavenworth gathered there and they had a choir. I developed a good relationship with the chorus director, Donna Griffith, who encouraged my love of music and gave me my first taste of singing in front of a live audience. She didn't know what to do with me–I was not a soprano or an alto. She ended up putting me in the back row. I remember feeling jealous at Christmastime, when Ms. Griffith picked another girl to sing the soprano solo for "O Holy Night." No doubt this inspired me: years later when I created my own Christmas album, I wrote and sang "O Night Divine."

By middle school, all I cared about was music. I was singing along to albums and jotting down my own songs on scraps of paper–little ditties that often rhymed.

The year I turned eleven, heading into the sixth grade, I began to get a lot of positive feedback from my music. I had been playing my three chords on my guitar, writing songs, and forming impromptu "bands" with different friends from school. With two of them, we decided to enter a talent contest–Bob Hammill was emcee–for the Leavenworth Plaza Talent Show one weekend. We didn't win, but we did come in second place, and boy, did that spur me on.

I remember the sheer joy and excitement of being up onstage, playing and singing out to the audience, completely unencumbered. All the holding back I had to do at home, all the suppressing of my feelings–all of it disappeared in an instant.

Something about me changed that night at the talent show. I decided that I was not only going to be a musician, but I was going to be a famous musician. My dream was to sing like Carole King on *Tapestry*, the first album my dad had ever bought me. I started to imagine hearing my own songs on the radio.

Though my mom was not very interested in hearing me play music and sing, her mother loved it! We often visited my grandparents, driving from Kansas to Arkansas for school vacations and holidays. I loved my grandmother Annie Lou, and while she never said anything aloud, as she was not someone who wore her emotions on her sleeve, I felt loved by her and trusted that she actually cared about me. As soon as I walked in the door, her small house fragrant with cakes or pies, she would say, "Come here, Missy, come here and play for me." Her encouragement and praise meant the world to me.

I took a poem from an old children's book of poetry, *The Good Little Sheep*, and put its refrain to the same chords Mr. Raymond had taught me—A, D, and E. I couldn't wait to go back to Arkansas and play it for her.

It was during my eleventh year, and we were visiting my grandmother more frequently. I didn't think of why that might be the case. On the way down, I thought of two things: playing "The Good Little Sheep" for Annie Lou and staying up as late as possible so Jenny fell asleep first.

On one trip, after supper at her house, I took my guitar into Annie Lou's bedroom, where she was lying down. She hadn't joined us for dinner; in fact, she hadn't gotten out of the bed at all during that visit. I pulled up a chair and I played my new song for her on my Stella guitar.

The good little sheep run quickly and soft
Their colors are gray and white
They follow their leader nose to tail
For they must be home by night

Oh, the song made her so happy! She loved it. She smiled at me from bed, even though it looked like it was painful to do so. Then she said in a whispery voice, "Oh, Missy, after I die, will you put those words in my casket?"

I was stunned. No one had even told me she was sick. No one ever mentioned the word "cancer."

Annie Lou died soon after.

On our way home that summer, our family stopped at a hotel in Eureka Springs. As usual, I had to share a room with Jenny. When she got too close to me in the bathroom, I bristled and said, "Don't you ever touch me again."

I did not know where my courage came from to stand up to Jenny. Maybe it was the raw grief I was feeling. Maybe I had channeled my grandmother's love for me. But all I knew was that some part of me had begun to come forth, and Jenny listened. She never physically—or sexually—touched me again.

When we went back to Arkansas for the funeral a few weeks later, I wrote down the words to the song and handed the piece of paper to my aunt Martha, my mother's sister. I explained to her my grandmother's request to be buried with the lyrics I wrote for her and asked that she place them in the casket for me.

I did not want to go to the viewing, afraid of what death had done to her sweet face.

"Please don't make me go," I said to my mother.

In my young life, I had just experienced my first loss, and it was the first time sadness touched me in such an acute way. It felt too big for me, this grief, like it could sweep me away on its tide.

When I returned to my home in Kansas, I sat outside on the front porch playing those three chords—A, D, and E. I reached down deep inside to a place raw with loss, and for the first time, I wrote from a very real feeling—not one that I imagined. I was just beginning to comprehend this source within me, a source I would later identify as creation. Back then, at eleven years old, it was simply a comfort. I wrote another song for my grandmother:

LONELY IS A CHILD

Trees are swaying in the wind
Things are so free
But I sit here waiting
For her to come home to me
Lonely is a child waiting for its mother
To come home
Lonely is a child waiting for its mother
But a mother has he none

I think often of Annie Lou, how graced I was by her unconditional acceptance and love. I've also often wondered about the chasm between that love and the love I didn't feel from my own mother, my grandmother's own daughter. It's a mystery I've never solved—having had an unknowable mother whose own mother gifted me an affection I craved. I understand it now as the universe's way of finding another way to reach me. I miss my grandmother to this day, but I do think that this first loss connected to me a place within where all my music comes from.

For years, I had convinced myself that my childhood was one of surviving my mother's cold distance and my sister's abuse. I had convinced myself that all of those pain points were part of my past, tucked away and no longer any of my concern. *Move on from the pain*, I unconsciously told myself—simple as that. I see now that, though music helped me begin to process complicated feelings and had the power to ease some of the pain and aloneness I was feeling, it was by no means eradicating it. Other than that one song I wrote after my grandmother died, I was really a young girl looking for attention and love. I'd had a taste from Annie Lou, and I got some from my father, but at a cost: my sister and mother resented me even more. Yes, my father and I had a special bond, one that was all about being on the road, loving music, and wanting to have some fun. But—and I'll speak for myself—I was escaping, not really dealing with the messy truth of my family's situation. My dad was likely doing the same. I had not yet integrated the significance of the tension between my parents, my mother's drinking to mute her deep unhappiness, Jenny's raging slide into alcohol and drugs, possibly as a cry for help through her own pain. While my dad and I created a life raft for ourselves, I see now that it was a reductive way to see the effect of those early years on all of us.

Now I knew that if I was really going to live in love—especially in love and forgiveness of myself—I could no longer wrap up my childhood story so neatly into absolutes; I had to truly acknowledge the pain, the injury, and the violation, which meant sitting in its truth and letting myself really feel it. After that summer night in LA, when I began this spiritual journey, that's what I had begun to do—love myself.

CHAPTER 3

DOUBLE CLICK

I love doing puzzles. I love laying out a thousand pieces of all different colors, shapes, and sizes and gradually making a picture emerge. The more complicated the better: landscapes, an array of books, maps of continents, images of the cosmos and galaxies, an impressionist painting. It's a kind of meditation for me.

When my hands are busy, my mind can drift. This is similar to how I begin to write music. I may or may not have lyrics in mind, but I start strumming on one of my guitars and let the song take shape. Just like the puzzle, I trust that my fingers are conversing with my brain, figuring it out.

Figuring out that I was gay was also a kind of puzzle-solving, a meandering process that took time, with some of the pieces just not fitting into the space provided.

Like many a teenager, I lived in a muddle of thoughts and feelings that were mostly all about me. Nothing wrong with that, of course. But an essential difference, one that I am now grateful for—especially observing my own kids trying to navigate adolescence and the teen years under a public microscope—is that I felt no pressure from the outside world. No one seemed remotely interested in my identity. I was a tomboy, a singer-songwriter. I was the high school history teacher's daughter. I was Jenny's younger sister. That's how I was viewed from the outside. All I wanted to do was focus on the image of me as singer-songwriter hell-bent on becoming a rock star.

Once I turned twelve, after our successful talent show, Mr. Hammill asked if my friends and I would be interested in being part of his variety show, which featured several acts and performed at a number of different venues around Leavenworth. Heck yeah!

My friends and I began doing shows and performing at local old folks' homes, the VA center, and at the four prisons in Leavenworth, including one performance we did at the Kansas state women's prison. I remember distinctly getting up on that stage wearing my jeans, cowboy boots, and semi-western shirt, and looking out at the fierce-looking group of women, their hair cut short or slicked back, their drab gray uniforms masking their identities. It was intimidating for all of a minute, but then, with all of the bravado of a seasoned professional, I sang my heart out. I loved being up there in front of a crowd with a mix of excitement and ease that had something to do with the intimacy with the audience. Being up onstage and connecting with myself in this new way gave me a burst of hope that my dream of becoming a rock star might actually happen.

Performing was its own reward, but I also loved getting paid for my music. I can still remember my first paid gig—for a Parents Without Partners event at the local Knights of Columbus. I was paid ten bucks in cash! I started saving my money from way back then and have never stopped. I loved marking down my deposits in my little savings account book given to me by the Leavenworth Savings and Loan and watching the numbers grow. I was a very busy little twelve-year-old.

That next year after my performance at the women's prison was when I was asked to join a country and western band, the Wranglers. I was lead vocals and sang classic country songs like "Stand By Your Man" and "Jackson." We performed songs by Tammy Wynette, Johnny Cash, and Loretta Lynn. I only played with the Wranglers a few months—after all, I was only thirteen and all the guys were in their twenties. It became clear that their including me was only temporary. I'm guessing now that they didn't want to be held back by a young girl who needed supervision as they ventured farther outside of Leavenworth to do shows.

But another band had heard me play around town and asked me to try out with them. The Showmen were a well-regarded band from St. Joseph, Missouri. They were playing at the Leavenworth NCO— the noncommissioned officers club, and asked me if I'd audition to see if I was a good fit to sing lead vocals.

The NCO had a reputation for being rowdy, a detail I didn't share with my mother.

The night of the live audition, I came down with the flu, and my mother did not want me to go. "You have a fever over one hundred!" I remember her saying.

But I was not going to let that stop me—this was my chance to play my biggest venue yet. I wanted to play for the band and see if they thought I was any good. I had something to prove, and being sick with a head cold was not going to get in my way. So my dad drove me over to the army base, and I did a quick audition and belted out "Stand By Your Man," which was becoming one of my staples. I got the job and began to perform more or less regularly with the Showmen. Since I wasn't yet eighteen, my dad had to drive me to the gigs, which were all over Kansas and Missouri.

The gigs were mostly on weekends, which meant my dad and I would head off in the family car, leaving my mom and Jenny at home, mad as hell at us and barely speaking to each other. My dad would try and get out in front of my mother's resentment by going to the liquor store before we left for a gig and leaving a bottle of vodka in a brown paper sack on the kitchen table for her. Admittedly, this was more to assuage his own guilt than it was to take care of my mother. I don't think he knew how to address my mother's unhappiness and growing dependence on alcohol. I see now that he was simply trying to placate her and keep the peace.

In the car, as we drove away, I could almost hear his sigh of relief as we put some distance between us and what was broken.

Around when I turned fourteen and had been singing and performing professionally for a couple of years, my father bought a Yamaha upright piano for the house. He said it was for my mother, who used to play the piano. I knew intuitively that he was trying to make amends for the fact that we were gone every weekend for shows and Wednesday nights for band practice. I still have that piano in my home and cherish it to this day.

Whenever I was home, I was on that piano, teaching myself how to play. I had long since stopped taking music lessons from Mr. Raymond, believing that I could teach myself. I wrote songs as I played, played as I wrote. I practiced covers I would perform with the band. When I taught myself the Janis Joplin song "Me and Bobby McGee," I discovered the one song my mom really liked to hear me play. She never asked me to play anything I wrote—with one exception, much, much later in my life, when she complimented me about "Chrome Plated Heart."

"The lyrics are very Zen. Your grandmother would be so proud," she said, in a moment of quiet reflection.

Looking back, I think playing a wide variety of music helped me to be open and curious, and able to trust what I heard in my head. I began to write down lyrics, play with rhythm and melody, making it up as I went, trusting my gut and following my heart. I loved the challenge to match music to lyrics and wrote songs and music with people listening in mind. Storytelling was always a big part of it. What I love about music and its power of conveying story is how the words work in conjunction with the music, with the beat, with the silences. Not everything needs to be expressed in words. Music itself carries so much of the meaning and does so much of the work. To me, it's the perfect way to tell a story: to allow for sound and the listener on the other side of it to fill in the meaning.

When I wasn't at a gig or practicing at home, I was finding another place to play and sing. When I heard that the Youth of the Chapel group (the YOC for short) at nearby Fort Leavenworth was staging the musical *Godspell*, which would be presented to all army service members and their families, I pleaded with them to let a kid from town be involved. They said I could play the guitar in the orchestra, but I had to join the youth group. That was easy, as I loved those kids. They were vibrant, open, and eager for whatever life had to offer. Soon, Sundays became YOC time. I played my weekend gigs on Friday and Saturday nights, got home super late, then was up early for eight a.m. church service. I even wrote a song called "Love in This Place" for YOC. It became a theme. I was feeling more and more like Reggie, my favorite character from the Archies!

By the time I turned sixteen, I had played professionally for four years, singing country and rock songs, often in the sanctuaries of alcohol and dancing of the Midwest. Some nights got wild. One night, I had to duck behind a Hammond B3 organ as bottles and chairs were being thrown. I watched as people in the audience became so intoxicated they'd fall into me as I performed. Once a guy fell into my mic stand, which hit me in the mouth and chipped my two front teeth. I saw firsthand that alcohol could make things ugly and was nothing to be desired. Between my home situation and what I witnessed while performing, I had no interest in alcohol. My dad didn't drink, either. Needless to say, these places were not ideal for a child. But I was getting in front of an audience and playing my music—that's all that mattered.

That summer, my father took me on a road trip to California—just the two of us. He wanted to visit his brothers and a sister. One brother lived in San Diego, and another brother and his sister lived in the Silver Lake area of LA. My dad and I both had time off in the summer, while my mom still had to work. Jenny had already left home at this point. She'd joined a motorcycle gang after she graduated from high school. I was thrilled to be doing a real road trip with my dad. Things always felt better when we were together, just the two of us, far away from my mom's brooding tension and whatever chaos Jenny was cooking up.

We drove west in his Cutlass ("Never buy a Ford, Missy—only a Chevy"), listening to music on his eight-track player: Cat Stevens, James Taylor, the Eagles, and John Denver. We sang the familiar songs together and discussed the lyrics. He helped me to see how storytelling worked through song lyrics.

It was my first time seeing LA, and the city felt like a crazy mishmash of colors—the bright green elegance of the palm trees and the steady stream of blue sky didn't seem to match the grittiness of Sunset Boulevard. I remember driving with the windows down, the Southern California sun warming my skin, and looking up through the windshield and seeing skywriting above, announcing a new song being released by Crosby, Stills & Nash! Suddenly a light bulb went off in my head—I knew that band—the mysterious CSN! Driving west down Sunset Boulevard, all I saw were signs of music: Tower Records, movie posters, giant billboards—music was everywhere. We drove by A&M Records, where I'd end up working in a few years. And my second thought? This was where I belonged. I could move here. I could live here. My fantasy about being a rock star and moving to LA started to take on more shape, the dream becoming almost tangible.

One of my favorite memories from that trip was driving the PCH, the road that hugs the Pacific Ocean, and eating at Gladstone's with my dad, Aunt Sue, and Uncle Carl. We sat at an outside table overlooking the ocean, ordered platters of shellfish, and gorged—on the food as much as the sprawling sea, the beach filled with sunbathers and surfers, and the overwhelming sensation that life was just much better here. I knew without him having to say it out loud, that my dad would move to California in a heartbeat if it weren't for my mom, who couldn't imagine making such a radical change to how she lived.

When we got back to Leavenworth, and I got ready to start my junior year of high school, I felt more determined than ever to do whatever I could to make my dream come true. Never a straight-A student—much to my mother's chagrin—I began to realize that academics were not my priority. Instead, I made the decision to use my mental energy for one purpose and one purpose only: create music.

I began writing songs in earnest. Most of them were full of intense longing and loneliness, a craving for love, a desire to be held, a desperate need to feel understood so I wouldn't feel so alone. I created stories and wrote songs about characters that captured those feelings—feelings that were too big for my own limited experiences. One of those songs was about a girl whose father was in prison—and how much she missed him even if he was a bad man. She visits him in prison, and the father tells her, "Don't make the same mistakes I made. Just run, run towards your dreams."

When I recently reread my lyric notebooks from those days, they were full of teenage angst and poetry, like I was circling the fortress of my heart, not wanting to get too close—probably out of fear. But there were signs of my confusion about my sexuality. Everyone comes to awareness on their own timeline, but I was still resistant.

An early entry shows it plainly: I had a crush on a kid named Melvin, but I was also obsessing about a girl named Jo, whom I had met at Christian youth summer camp. She wanted to be friends with me, but I nervously backed off—not ready to get close to my own feelings. I have no idea if she was interested in me romantically, but I think I had those intentions for her. Not knowing where to put those intentions, I instead wrote about her in my diary. *Circling the fortress, afraid to get close.*

Then one day during my junior year of high school after Social Studies class let out, my teacher asked me to stay back for a few minutes. Her name was Mrs. D'Angelo. She was thin, with really short hair like Helen Reddy.

I sat down, feeling a bit nervous and curious. I was never in any trouble—so I couldn't imagine what she wanted to talk with me about.

Then Mrs. D'Angelo said she wanted to tell me a story about a girl she'd gone to college with who she'd really loved a lot. They spent all of their time together, listening to music, hanging out, studying together at the library. One day, the girl called my teacher and told her she wanted to play a special song over the phone—the Beatles' "And I Love Her."

I was listening intently, not sure why my teacher was telling me this story. Was she telling me something about herself? Did she know something about me that I didn't know myself?

I gathered my books and the mess of my teenage questions and practically ran out of the room. How dare she see me!

In the days after that encounter, I kept wondering about the conversation. I knew Mrs. D'Angelo was married. She didn't seem to be talking about me. Or was she? I still wasn't sure what it all meant, but my sense was that Mrs. D'Angelo was somehow trying to tell me something, like she was in my corner—though I wasn't sure what corner I was in!

Of course, years later I saw more clearly that Mrs. D'Angelo was reaching out trying to let me know that I was not alone, that it was okay to be gay. At the time, I wasn't quite putting two and two together. I didn't know anyone who was gay. There were no obvious gay people in my high school. And Leavenworth certainly didn't have a gay neighborhood!

I think part of my not having a name for what was going on with me was because there were so few gay role models—especially gay women in the late 1970s—and there were certainly no out entertainers. I had no one person to look up to, no one person to reflect me back to me. Mine is not an unusual story in this regard.

Meanwhile, I was dating guys. A year earlier, at the end of my sophomore year, I had gotten together with a guy named Mark, who was two years older. He was a senior at the time and getting ready to leave Leavenworth to go away to college. He was a sax player and heard me perform at school. He invited me to join his band and play piano and sing vocals. He said he loved my deep voice and that he and his two bandmates really wanted me to sing "Sir Duke" by Stevie Wonder for a gig at the local VFW.

When we played "Sir Duke" I leaned into the piano keys, pulling on my image of Stevie Wonder but adding my own twist. The old-timers in the audience were whooping and hollering, and I just had a big fat smile on my face. We brought down the house! My bandmates were thrilled, telling me they finally had a vocalist who could do the song justice.

Mark was a senior and I was a sophomore, and we floated into a relationship—and I was relieved to have a boyfriend and be someone's girlfriend. Maybe I was not so different after all?

My friends seemed impressed that Mark and I were so tight. I was definitely curious about sex—but I remember feeling like I was traveling outside of my body, as if I were looking down on myself, whenever we fooled around. I was not even remotely aware of what this distance meant. I understand it now as a mild form of dissociation, which is a way of not dealing with unresolved feelings so we separate ourselves from the experience. But in the back of my mind, I think I was aware that Mark did not make my heart sing the way I imagined it could.

Mark must have felt my distance at some level, and one day told me that he'd been reading Dear Abby, the advice column that was published daily in most newspapers across the country. He said the column was about women who were frigid—as in, not into sex. He didn't say much more, but clearly, he was talking about me, implying that I had some kind of problem.

Then one night when we were hanging out, I told him about my dream to become a rock star—I remember feeling a bit nervous to be so open about something that was so personal and so important to me.

As I looked up at him, assuming he would totally understand where I was coming from, that he may even share a similar dream, he said, "Well, that's all fine and good, but when I get married, I want my wife to stay at home."

Click.

After that night, I pulled away from him big-time, without hesitation and without really saying much to him. In some ways, my withdrawal from that relationship was a retreat to protect myself from getting hurt. He didn't seem to like me all that much. But deep down, I knew he wasn't what I wanted, either. I did feel hurt by his implied criticism, but I know now that it was the larger issue that was so offending. This wasn't about me, it was about the larger cultural messages we girls received. Were we wrong to follow our dreams? Why did mine seem so outlandish? I'd hear my mother's voice, admonishing me: "Oh, Missy, don't get your hopes up." Things hadn't changed much since she'd been a girl.

Back then, my mother was talking about my music, but it felt like she was talking about me—*Missy, don't get your hopes up—no one will ever like you. No one will ever make the aching loneliness go away.* I realize in hindsight that she was really talking to herself, but at the time, what I'd heard in my heart was *no one will ever love you.*

On the other hand, I could not imagine myself being someone's wife or getting married, much less having children—at least not in the way the options were at the time. I seemed to know that about myself. So where did that leave me?

When Mark went off to college at the end of the summer, I did not shed any tears—I only felt more determined to make my way in the world on my own terms, which meant becoming not only a rock star, but a rock star who would never have to depend on someone else financially. I was determined to be independent and prove my mom and Mark wrong.

It was during that same summer my dad and I took the trip to LA, after which I turned to my music, happy to pour myself into writing songs, many of them with an *I'm so very sad and alone* theme.

I was often sad and often alone. I just didn't understand where the line was. Was I just a regular teenager feeling moody and up-set with my mom? Hating my sister, whose bad behavior seemed to have tarnished our family's reputation in our small town? I didn't know why I felt so uneasy.

Truth is, I liked being alone in my basement, writing songs and playing my guitar. Sure, I had a lot of friends—but they knew me as the spunky girl who played guitar and sang in the youth choir. They did not know the real me—*I* didn't know the real me. But I tried to convince myself I was okay with it.

At the beginning of my junior year, a new boy came to our high school. His parents were in the army and transferred to Leaven-worth. Jeff was tall, blond, and handsome, and we sat next to each other in history. He was also a star football player of our high school football team. More shocking than that, he asked me to the fall homecoming dance.

To say I was surprised is an understatement. I was popular, and not unattractive, but I was also a total tomboy and known for being Missy the musician. I was super outgoing and friendly, especially to anyone who was new to school, so maybe that attracted him.

One of my good friends even said to me, "I can't believe he asked you." Emphasis on "you." Geez.

My mom was, relatively speaking, ecstatic. A football player had asked me to a dance! I think I remember her smiling at me when I told her the news, and for an instant, I thought maybe she'd changed her mind about me. Jenny had been gone for a while with the motorcycle gang, and I dared to hope that my mom might show an interest in me now that Jenny wasn't around to keep her on edge with worry or anger. After my being invited to the prom by a star football player, I thought just maybe things would be better between me and my mom.

As the date approached, I began to think about a dress, my hair, and did I really have to wear makeup? I had never paid any attention to these "girly" things. But now I seemed to be part of a script: going to the high school dance with the star of the football team—no doubt the fantasy of many a Kansas girl!

By the time the night of the big dance came, I was super excited. I had chosen a dress, my mom had helped me with my hair, and I even put on some eye shadow—probably blue. I remember my mom took pictures of me that night, which made me feel special.

Jeff came to the door and awkwardly handed me a clunky corsage for my wrist. I gave him a white rose boutonniere to put on the lapel of his tuxedo.

He looked very handsome, his tan corduroy suit matching his khaki-colored eyes, his blond hair framing a strong jaw. He was about a foot taller than me, and I found myself enjoying looking up at him.

I loved that he played football—I was a Kansas City Chiefs fan even back then and had been watching them with my dad for years. I figured we could talk about football when we weren't dancing.

We got to the prom, but instead of mingling with the other kids in our class, Jeff wanted to sit in the bleachers. I assumed he was feeling shy.

We started to chat about where he'd moved from and how Leavenworth was different. I kept looking over at the kids dancing, and every time a good song came on, I looked expectantly at my date, who seemed to have no interest in the dance floor.

We kept talking, with me practicing my conversation skills.

Song after song. Finally I said, "C'mon, let's dance!"

He said, "No, I can't."

"What do you mean you can't? Like you don't know how? That's okay—we can fake it and just have fun."

And he said, "No, I can't. Dancing is against my religion."

It turned out his father was a preacher who believed dancing was a sin.

So there I was, all dressed up and stuck on the bleachers with Mr. Beautiful.

After the dance, Jeff drove me home, walked me to the front door, and very matter-of-factly put out his hand for me to shake. "Good night, Missy," he said.

As he turned to go, I asked him, "Why did you ask me to the dance?"

"I thought you were the safest person to ask so I wouldn't be tempted to sin."

Ouch. That stung.

I didn't let on, but a private shame burned inside.

But over the summer, as I mulled over my two short romances, I grew curious that my bad luck with guys didn't seem to affect me much; I hadn't sulked or cried over the loss of either Mark or Jeff, which made me wonder if there was something wrong with me. Weren't girls supposed to be sad and disappointed when a boy didn't like them? Why didn't I seem to care?

Double click.

READY TO LOVE

The yearning I had wondered about was fully at my door. I had witnessed men and women holding each other on the dance floor for years. I didn't want to be one of those women, but there was something I couldn't quite put my finger on, something just out of my reach. It was there when I sang the songs. I could feel a different kind of energy come out in my voice and a strumming passion when I played my guitar more ferociously.

Desire was making itself known to me, but I didn't quite know for what.

And then I met Jane, the colonel's daughter.

Jane and I were friends, even best friends by high school standards. We went to parties together. We drove into Kansas City together. We spent afternoons in my basement listening to records or watching movies. We even got jobs at the local KFC, working side by side.

To the outside world, she and I were close friends, but I began to feel like there was something more going on between us. All I wanted to do was hang out with her.

For a while, we continued the charade that there was not this other tension between us. Then, on the night of my seventeenth birthday, when I was staying at her house, in the quiet of her bedroom, we began to kiss.

And then it clicked for real.

Kissing a girl unleashed a raw, wonderful rush of hormonal lust and excitement. Like a torrent of heat that raced through me. Suddenly my body was hungry for touch. Hungry for connection. The mix of lust and love was intoxicating and at the same time unsettling. I didn't know anyone in Leavenworth who was gay. Was I automatically gay now that I'd kissed a girl? I was excited and trepidatious all at once.

In a dramatic declaration, I told my parents that I was taking a break from music because I wanted to have fun my senior year. What I didn't say out loud was that I was consumed with Jane and our relationship. All I could think about was this sexual awakening within me. It was visceral energy that was so strong, so powerful, I could not think of anything else.

I had always been a physical person—I liked sports, and put enormous physicality into playing the guitar. I enjoyed being in sync with my body when I performed and felt the energy build in my muscles as I moved around the stage. But sex? Sex was a whole new level of physical, and it became almost a hunger that seemed insatiable, bottomless.

Throughout my senior year, Jane and I were inseparable. I tried to wrap my head around this very clear information: I was gay. I preferred girls to boys. I was, after all, different from most people I'd known.

At first, I didn't really feel burdened by this information about myself. It was my secret. All I wanted to do was revel in the sheer exhilaration of being in my body and making more sense to myself—and, of course, the thrill of kissing and touching Jane and being kissed and touched by Jane.

You know when you discover something new about yourself? You just want to sit in the new awareness, feel it, get to know it so that it's so familiar you no longer have to think about it—it just is?

My relationship with Jane was not all love and laughter, far from it. She was jealous of my other friends and didn't like it if I wanted to do anything except hang out together. If I brought up music, which I was beginning to miss, she would look at me as if I had just threatened her.

She was also volatile and moody. She seemed endlessly on the edge of anger, jealousy, a clawing need for attention. I was right in there with her, always willing to placate her feelings, always trying to make her feel better, safer, loved. I remember thinking: *If she's so jealous, she must really love me.*

I didn't like to fight and avoided even the whisper of conflict. I'd had a lot of practice assuming the role of steady presence, the one offering the listening ear, the willingness to weather the storm of another's emotions. I slipped right into that self-assigned role—one I'd played out in my childhood to perfection. I liked this image of myself—strong, not needy, above the fray. Of course, this required that I sit on my own feelings, detach from myself, and stay focused on her.

No surprise, this became a pattern that would show up in many of my future relationships. I'd let my lover take center stage with her needs and feelings, while quietly ignoring my own. At a deeper level, this willingness to take the back seat, even accepting physical abuse—Jane struck me across the face a few times in fits of jealous rage—was also a reflection of a disturbing belief that something was wrong with me. And adding to this shame was the deeply familiar tension between violation and connection rooted in my relationship with my sister, a tangled confusion it would take me years to unravel and understand.

Many of my friends who I met later in Boston and then in LA came out back in the late '70s and '80s internalized this same sense of homophobia, with an unconscious attitude of *I'll take what I can get* compromising our choice of partners and relationships themselves. I was not at all conscious of this silent agreement, but much later, after two big relationships that included the births of my four children, and having ultimately, finally created a relationship of love, mutual respect, and integrity, I see now that so many of my early relationships were founded on the belief that I was undeserving of more. I know it's not that simple, but it helps me to understand my part in their dysfunction.

As women back then, we weren't taught to hold each other up. I see how despite my daughters' almost-ten years age difference both have a more evolved understanding of their own worth and how it's not tied to either gender or sexuality. We still have a long way to go, but I trust that we are progressing in the right direction.

When I was young, I didn't have a model for the kind of supportive, truly intimate and secure romantic relationship I wanted. I didn't even know what that partnership could look like. Like so many gay women and men of my generation and generations before me, I didn't have the opportunity to observe loving relationships of all kinds. Without knowing what was possible, without knowing there were millions of other people like me, I defaulted to the thought: *This is all I have.*

READY TO LOVE

When I look at you all I can see
Is the shadow of your life
You see this stage is a mirror
You can see me
But I can't see past its light
Lovers have tried to reach down inside
I only said that they were wrong
But when all I've got left is me and my pride
I realize you can't buy love with a song
So somebody take me out of the night
Show me what life is made of
Won't somebody reach inside of my heart
I think that I'm ready to love
I think that I'm ready to love
I feel like I'm ready to love

A BEELINE FOR BOSTON

My parents were adamant about me going to college, but all that I was interested in studying was music. Earlier in high school, my mom made me take voice lessons, classical piano, and music theory. She signed me up for classes at the University of Missouri, Kansas City, and drove me out there on weekends for lessons. I sat and listened to a professor go on about theory and couldn't have been more bored. It had nothing to do with what I was interested in. I wanted to play sports—basketball and volleyball—and be in the marching band. But my mom insisted that I should have a background in classical music. I understand now this was her way of participating in my musical education. And, while I can appreciate from here the efforts she made, it felt like she was pushing me to be a musician the way that she wanted me to be a musician with no consideration for who I was. I didn't feel seen by her. I wish this had been something I could have told her, but the need for that conversation was solved for me. One dreary Saturday, the professor approached me after class and said, "Missy, tell your mother to save her money. You're going to sing the way you sing."

Relieved to have those classical music lessons come to an end, I focused on my own style.

Not one to give up lightly, my mom began pressuring me to study music at college. Both she and my dad encouraged me to consider Juilliard, Eastman, Oberlin, and other classical music schools—but all of them would only let me study classical guitar, something that didn't appeal to me at all. The only college that was open to my interest in singing more popular music and playing acoustic and electric guitar was the Berklee College of Music in Boston, so I applied and was accepted.

Jane was pissed off and resentful that I was leaving Leavenworth. She had no plans; I had big plans; and the closer we got to graduation, the more volatile and moody she became. The relationship was coming to an end, and I welcomed the separation college would bring.

By late spring, I committed to going to Berklee. I've always loved learning and was thrilled by the idea that school was going to be all about playing music and studying what was most important to me.

My mom gave me a suitcase for my graduation—no doubt a

well-intentioned gift, but one that smarted. *Here you go—bye, bye.* Mad inside, I wanted to leave on my terms, not hers. I began packing my bags and counting the days when I'd be on my own in Boston, absorbed in my music. I was more than ready to leave Leavenworth behind.

You know when the universe seems to be listening? Giving you signs that you're being taken care of? That someone has their eye on you? Or that you sense, without knowing why, what's going to happen next? Or in talking with a friend you have a clear intuition about what he or she is going to say next? And you're right? Well, that was starting to happen. Synchronicities.

I've had many such instances in my life, but an early one was when I met my Berklee roommate, Helene, from New York City. Not only was she Jewish (I had never met a Jewish person before) but also a lesbian! Outspoken, smart, funny, and totally cool, Helene welcomed me to Boston with open arms, and I was thrilled. She had come to Berklee to study the violin—though she appeared to be nothing like the studious violin players that I knew of. Helene was that classic New Yorker—brazen and fearless, on the one hand, and amazingly frank about her own vulnerabilities—she seemed like a walking contradiction, and I loved her for it.

She was also my gateway to the gay scene in Boston.

In 1979, Boston had some pretty hip gay and lesbian bars and clubs—like Estelle's, the Rat, Jacques' Cabaret, and Somewhere Else, which were safe places for gays and lesbians to congregate and feel open about who we were. From the managers down to the bartenders, we were one big, chummy community where we all felt like we belonged. Up to that point, I had never stepped foot inside a gay club or bar—so these clubs were just short of intoxicating.

I was barely eighteen years old, and walking into a bar where men were dancing with men, where women were crowded together, arms around each other—it struck me like a lightning bolt, setting off every nerve cell in my brain and body.

Today there are so few true gay or lesbian bars or clubs—partly a reflection of the assimilation of LGBTQ+ people into our larger culture—but in the 1980s and even '90s, these bars and clubs were crucial to our community and to so many of us individually.

And I was thrilled to be part of it, moving into myself in a new way. I didn't try to make my voice sound higher. I wore the clothes I wanted to wear, which had a Midwestern flair. But since I was never that into fashion, I perfected a kind of uniform—black boots, baggy jeans, and black motorcycle jacket. Just being inside these places made me relax and smile. These were my people.

At Berklee I didn't feel the same way. There was a formal tone to the classes and an unspoken rule that we had to take ourselves, jazz, and our careers very seriously. Frankly, all I wanted to do was hang out with Helene and go to the gay bars.

About midway through the fall semester, Jane called to say she missed me and she wanted to move to Boston.

I was surprised and not exactly excited, but I smothered my feelings and told her, "Great." I didn't want to say more, afraid that she'd get angry and start a fight.

Without considering how her moving in with me would work, I let it happen. As soon as she arrived with her overflowing suitcase, it became alarmingly clear that she couldn't live with Helene and me in our room at Berklee. So what does a problem-solver do? She moves out of her dorm and finds a small apartment and then gets a job so she can pay the rent. I got a job as a security guard at a research hospital in Jamaica Plain, a town about six subway stops outside of the Back Bay. I barely made any money—and it was dreadfully boring. Still, I put my blinders on and just showed up.

One evening, as I began my commute by train at the Park Street T stop, a guitarist was busking. Something about how the sound refracted off the tunnels and walls of the underground station sounded beautiful, and I had an idea! A lot of Berklee musicians busked, so I said to myself, *Well, why don't I give it a try.* I liked the idea of playing for tips. The next evening was free, so I set myself up in the T station and started playing my first twelve string guitar (which eventually got stolen from the back of my car a few years later). My little hat started filling up with dollar bills. I loved all of it: the zig and zag of the commuters; the loud hissing of the trains; the dank smells from the tracks—it all felt so real and yet romantic at the same time. There I was playing to small groups of assembled commuters who hummed in recognition of a song, which just made me play harder. I played "Me and Bobby McGee," "Please Come to Boston," and George Benson's "On Broadway." I had a blast.

It also made me realize how much I'd missed performing!

By the end of that night, I'd made more money than I would have in three days working at the hospital!

I busked a few more times, loving the downtown grunge of the Park Street station on the Green Line, the closeness to my audience. I needed people to hear my music! I went through the newspaper to see what places offered live music; I got a list together and started showing up, asking if they were interested in hearing me perform. Some of the managers and owners of the restaurants and bars dismissed me outright. Others shrugged and said they had all the musicians they needed. But I struck luck at Ken's by George, a new restaurant that had a bar and was trying to cater to the yuppie set taking over Back Bay and downtown Boston. A seafood restaurant on Dartmouth and Claremont, it was a nice place near my apartment on Hereford. I did a quick audition, and the manager hired me immediately for the early shift, five to nine p.m.

I sang popular covers from Barry Manilow, Billy Joel, Barbra Streisand, and Neil Diamond—and some show tunes from *Cabaret*, and *Funny Girl*—all the favorites that my dad and I listened to. After a month, I was promoted to the later, and more lively shift, from nine to midnight. How I loved it! I was back in front of a live audience, but this time, they weren't throwing beer bottles and darts or waiting to board a train. They were a more sophisticated crowd, who presented a new kind of challenge: How do I connect with a room of couples and businesspeople wanting to chat and enjoy their cocktails? They didn't come to Ken's by George to hear music—I just happened to be there. But I was determined to understand how to read this new audience and connect with them. I needed their attention.

Meanwhile, things were not going so well with Jane. She didn't like that I went to school during the day; she didn't like that I performed at Ken's at night; she didn't like that I sometimes went out to the clubs and met other women.

Jane had arrived with no plans for her future, and I was beginning to see that she didn't have any ambitions. She wanted my full attention, which I couldn't give her, nor did I want to. I was not motivated to drop everything to make her happy like I used to in high school. I was growing and learning and living a new life and had so many other things on my mind: college, my set list for Ken's, and oh, the women I was starting to meet and flirt with at the bars and clubs around town.

One night I met Caroline at one of the girl bars near where I lived. We lingered at the bar, flirted a lot, and kept drinking. When I got home, Jane came up to me and slapped me across the face.

That one slap brought back her jealous rages from when we both lived in Leavenworth.

I looked at her as I put my hand to my face to feel the burn. I needed the hot sensation to get up the gumption to tell Jane that she had to leave.

* * *

One night as I was playing at Ken's, I noticed one of my Berklee professors sitting in the audience. I was nervous but determined to play my best. I did a couple of my usual covers, and then got up my courage to sing and play an original song, which I hadn't done since the talent show back in Leavenworth when I was eleven. I put my heart and soul into my performance. When it was over, I expected my professor to come up to me or give me a signal of recognition or acknowledgment.

Nope.

Honestly, I don't think he even knew who I was.

That was another signal from the universe: despite its reputation, Berklee was not for me, and I was not for Berklee.

I realized that my passion was performing and writing and playing my own music. That's what got me going; that's what made me feel most alive.

I dropped out.

By that time, I was attracting a regular audience for my shows at Ken's. I wouldn't call it a following, but I began to see more and more women who may or may not–wink, wink–have known I was gay. But they sure were.

Then what happened?

I got fired.

Not giving me much of a reason, the manager just said it was time for me to move on. I've always been convinced that he did not like the steady stream of lesbians that seemed to be coming to the bar.

I moved on and quickly got a job at a new restaurant and bar that was opening in Copley Plaza, but the day before I was supposed to start, the place burned down.

At one point in the midst of all this fitful, go-nowhere searching, a couple of Wiccans read my cards at a bar where I was working. I remember, clear as day, one of the women saying to me, "You're going to be very successful . . . You're going to have four children."

A mother of four kids? That's never going to happen. I'm going to be a gay rock star!

I decided my time in Boston had come to a close.

*   *   *

I never had any notion of staying long term back in Leavenworth. Kansas was a halfway stop on my way to LA, besides I didn't have enough to tie me to Boston and felt rattled by getting fired and the new place burning down. But I needed some time to regroup, so I moved back in with my parents to save money. I got a job at the local youth center, teaching art and drama activities. I began reaching out to some of my high school friends who didn't go to college and most of whom worked at the Hallmark candle factory.

I got involved with a woman I knew from the youth center. She was younger than me by a couple of years, and I was the first woman she'd been with. She was pretty chill and, unlike Jane, no drama—easy and fun to be with.

Without really thinking about it, I brought her home one night. When I got up the next morning, my mother had left me a note:

I don't know the nature of your psychological illness, but do not bring that girl over here anymore. If you're going to continue this behavior, you can't live in this house.

Pain seared through me, and I felt about an inch high—humiliated, ashamed, and suddenly unwanted in my own home.

In the days that followed, I realized that I could no longer live at home. I didn't really want to see my mom's face, filled with disgust and scorn. I moved out...

I had a strong relationship with the pastor of our church, where I had spent so much time—volunteering and attending church retreats. He was a mentor I could trust. I had believed in the Christian teachings; God made sense to me. But hate and shame didn't seem to fit in with what Jesus was saying.

I explained to the pastor what my mom had written to me and that I was no longer welcome at home. I wanted to be truthful, so I said, "I'm gay. I don't think that's going to change."

He took my hand gently and said, "There are probably some people in this church who would say that it's wrong for you to love another woman. That it's a sin. But I can't go along with them on that way of thinking. I can't believe God would have invented a love that could be wrong."

He then encouraged me to trust myself and believe that I had what it takes to be on my own. To this day, I am grateful for his kind guidance.

His support helped me decide to move out of my parents' house and to go live in Kansas City. I still had an LA plan in my mind, but I wanted to work a bit more and save some money. I also wanted to see if I was ready to start playing live again.

I auditioned at a bar and restaurant called La Veranda Lounge. A cabaret-like atmosphere with a strong gay overtone made me feel right at home.

As in Boston, I got hired for the early shift, but after a week, the manager fired the guy who played the late-night set, and I took over.

I rented a small apartment—literally a garret with no window—and suddenly felt like a real musician out on my own.

I played nights, slept in late, got up and went immediately to my guitar and started writing songs. Some were a little maudlin, but there was a searching quality to them. I was making my dream of being a working musician come alive.

After about a month or so of living in a windowless apartment, my dreams of California took on a heightened intensity. Soon it was all I could think about. I started to plan my trip. I tried to research LA clubs and music producers, and record companies through the music magazines, but pre-internet, there was not a lot you could find out without being on the ground.

Before I pulled up stakes, I had one last thing I needed to do.

I went to see my dad. We'd always been so close, and I wanted to be able to tell him about my plan to move to California. I also wanted to tell him directly about being gay.

In an awkwardly formal way, I called and asked him if I could talk to him. I drove to our house and walked in the front door as if I were a stranger. My mom was at work, so it was just the two of us.

We sat down in the living room.

I was wringing my hands as I sat there next to him and tried to look him in the eye, but my own eyes kept drifting to my lap. Then I began to ramble, "Dad, I want to talk to you. I have something to tell you."

Struggling to find the right words, I blurted out, "There's something I need to say. I don't know how you're going to feel about it, but I'm kind of afraid to tell you." I was babbling.

"I'm homosexual," I finally said in a rush.

Even to my own ears, the word "homosexual" sounded too clinical, like I was giving myself a diagnosis.

My dad looked up at me, his face kind and placid, and said, "Is that all? I've got to say that I don't quite understand it, but as long as you're happy. I love you."

My being gay definitely did not feel like a choice, but I wasn't going to argue. He didn't hate me, so I took that and clung to it. I was very relieved.

All I wanted was to get the heck out of Leavenworth and never look back.

I was ready to roll. I was no longer Missy from Leavenworth. I was now Melissa Etheridge, driven to make a name for myself in the wilds of California—true California dreamin'. I couldn't get there fast enough.

*   *   *

Coming out in the 1980s was very different than it is now. I can't say I ever felt endangered or threatened, and I consider myself lucky. What I do have in common with many people who come out—even today, as our community has become more inclusive—is that when you feel different from the majority, when you internalize that difference as a negative, you buy into a shame cycle that is hard to stop.

But now, through this new lens of practicing a life of Spirit, I realize that in hiding my sexual orientation, I did buy into the shame of being gay, of being different from the ubiquity of heteronormative messages. Those bars that felt so exciting back in Boston were underground; we all shared an unspoken pact not to reveal who we really were to the world. Because what happened when we did? We got fired. Getting fired didn't break my heart, but it did cause that inner shame to surface, triggering the familiar self-doubt about who I was, who I am. Could I have told Jane to not come to Boston and ended that relationship before giving her another chance to strike me? Yes. But I didn't yet have enough self-awareness to see that I was engaged in self-betrayal. When I received my mom's blatantly scornful and shaming letter, I could no longer deny her distaste and scorn. Yes—my pastor and my dad were a comfort, but as we know, as humans, we tend to remember the negative more than the positive. So when I headed west, I was driven by my ambition but also by a need to escape the pain and humiliation from my mother's rejection. I didn't want anyone to know that I was wounded. I would continue to hide behind a veiled image of myself, so the people I'd meet in sunny California would never suspect that I wasn't a totally together, totally lovable chick from Kansas who was going to rock that town.

CHAPTER 4

WAITING ON A DREAM

The summer of '82, I drove west from Kansas to California on my own, determined to put all that came before behind me—the burdens of my childhood, my attempts to be a so-called normal girl and date guys, my brief stint in Boston—and to chart a new life for myself. I had three hundred dollars in my wallet as I set out for LA.

I'd saved to buy a brand-new car: a 1982 Mercury LN7—a sporty 1980s yellow hatchback. I absolutely loved that car. It had a 1.6-liter two-barrel engine with a lot of guts. The car had AC (a first for me) and a cassette player, and I'd sprung for JBL speakers. I'd made a box of cassettes and couldn't wait to blast my music with the windows rolled down—Stevie Nicks's *Bella Donna* album, Joan Armatrading, and Tom Petty.

I had mapped out my route on one of those oversized atlases that sat next to me on the passenger seat. I knew where I was going, following the same route my dad and I had taken that summer we drove from Kansas to LA years before.

I had planned out all of my stops—Oklahoma City, Amarillo,

Albuquerque, Phoenix, LA. In Oklahoma City I stayed with some folks I knew from Christian youth camp. They were like family to me, making me feel welcome right away, but also asking me why I was going to California: "Isn't California like granola—just fruits and nuts?"

I just smiled, nodded, and said, "Yup—just the way I like it."

In Amarillo, I stayed in a small hotel with a cowboy statue out front, which I remembered from my trip with my dad. When I got to Albuquerque, I checked into a Best Western. It was Friday night by then, so after dropping all my stuff in the room—my two guitars, speakers, an amp, and a couple of suitcases—I went to the lobby restaurant and took a seat at the bar. I enjoy talking to strangers, and it's easy for me to fall into a patter—the same way I do when I'm onstage.

That night, I began chatting with the bartender.

"Do you know a different type of bar? One that I might like?" I was trying that old closet trick, hoping he'd understand me via telepathy.

Clearly not, because he sent me to a super-straight bar. As I scanned the crowd, which was definitely not like me, I asked one of the waitresses if she knew a bar that someone like me would enjoy. Again, a little vague. But this time it worked. She drew a map on a paper napkin and said, "Look for the blue light above the door."

That was the women's bar in town. No name. Side street. Blue light above the door. I sat down at the bar and started talking to Dawn, the head bartender, who was as chatty as I was. By the end of the night, with a few beers in me, I said to her, "I'm going to be famous one day!"

For years, every time I traveled that route, I stopped at the Blue Light to play.

By the time I moved through Phoenix and made my way across the last bit of desert, I was welcomed to LA by rush-hour traffic.

I had just turned twenty-one, and thought I knew it all—and crazy as it sounds, I drove without fear, all adrenaline and determination. I was finally independent from my parents, and eager to meet other women like me. I instinctively felt that LA was a place where I could be myself—professionally and personally. I was absolutely determined to make it.

Doubts crept in. When the music faded to the background and my mind began to drift, I'd think to myself, *What's my story going to be? I'm just a girl from Kansas—am I really going to hit it big?*

I'd shake my head and just keep driving. As if ambition were gasoline, I was pressing on that pedal with a fury.

GOTTA WORK

I went to stay with my aunt Sue, my dad's sister, and soon discovered that my dad's two brothers—my uncles Carl and George—were . . . gay! No wonder my dad didn't seem to blink when I came out to him. Just sitting across from these dapper older men made me sigh with relief. People I could recognize.

My three hundred bucks wasn't going to last very long, so I immediately started looking for work, and just like I did back in Boston, I scanned the Calendar section of the *Los Angeles Times* for bars and clubs that offered live music. I got a gig at the Candy Store, an all-Black cabaret on Sunset Boulevard. I didn't make a dime, but I got to play—and shake hands with Stevie Wonder. That was such an LA thing—to bump into people on their way up ... or down.

Then I got hired at the Pink Flamingo, a women's bar in Silver Lake, near where my aunt lived. I played there a few weeks, but the money wasn't great. I did meet a woman who I asked out on a date. Running low on cash, I had to pawn my typewriter in order to pay for the date.

Terry lived in Long Beach, a beach town south of LA, so after I picked her up, we went to a women's bar called the Executive Suite, which used to be a steakhouse and had an old piano in the corner. The look and feel of the place was a welcoming mix of cool and laid-back ... and very lesbian.

When I had first encountered the gay bar scene in Boston, this Kansas girl was a bit scared until I made friends. The leather scene was unlike anything I'd ever seen back home. Really butch guys dressed head to toe in black leather or latex alongside drag queens, and a few random men in business suits. The scene was still underground, and I didn't quite know what to make of it.

But in California, things were different! There were men's bars and women's bars. The men's bars were all about dancing—disco was still raging. The women's clubs were more subtle—some had dancing, like at the Executive Suite, which was super popular then. But the other women's bars in Long Beach were smaller, clubs with no live music.

Well, I was going to change that.

A few nights after that first date, I went back to the Executive Suite and asked if I could play—my kind of *let me audition for you.* They hired me on the spot, and I started playing five nights a week and making twenty-five dollars a night for a five-to-nine p.m. set—real money to me then!

Within a few months, I had almost singlehandedly created a small music scene in Long Beach.

My relationship with Terry had come to an abrupt end when she discovered that I had enjoyed a few one-night stands with women I'd met at the bar—not something I'm very proud of, by the way—and I was more or less living out of my car. In my twenties, I would definitely describe myself as an enthusiastic dater, more into the chase than a real relationship. I soon discovered that Long Beach had a lot of options! There was something manageable about it. It didn't have the oversized flash and sparkle of LA, and maybe that's why I settled into it for a bit. Long Beach made me feel comfortable and relaxed. The clubs were small. The women were right there—out, proud, and welcoming.

There was also a trickle-down effect from Cal State, Long Beach, where a number of feminist academics were developing a thriving department, which eventually became the college's Women's, Gender & Sexuality Studies program. The work they were doing influenced many of the women I was hanging out with and I welcomed reading again—as if I were catching up on what I had missed in college. Even for the short time I spent at Berklee, the curriculum was all music, and my high school back in Leavenworth definitely did not have a women's studies class. I was into it and curious to know more.

My new friends recommended some of the big feminist authors from the '70s, including Kate Millett (*Sexual Politics*) and Shulamith Firestone (*The Dialectic of Sex*). Some of academic feminist theory was a bit intense for me, but I could appreciate the importance of their work on behalf of women. At that point, I had never really felt constrained by the fact that I was a woman. They also introduced me to some of the great lesbian poets—Adrienne Rich and Audre Lorde—whose precise and nuanced use of language captured the age-old struggle of women to be seen for who we are, not through a critical lens meant to constrain and demoralize. I read about the extent of how our culture objectifies women and socializes young girls to deny them opportunities and limit the scope of their dreams. I thought about Mark and all of the boys and men like him. It made me realize how my mother's unhappiness and frustration came from something so much larger than our individual family's experience and helped me to have compassion for her.

One of my favorite books from that time was Barbara Ehrenreich and Deirdre English's *Witches, Midwives & Nurses: A History of Women Healers*, a book about how throughout history women have always been healers, "wise women," though uncelebrated and marginalized.

Looking back, I should not be surprised that I was drawn to a book that was about feminism and healing!

This awakening to women's history and to the ongoing quest for equal rights pushed my ability to believe in my own experience and trust my feelings and way of seeing and being in the world. I began to apply this newfound insight into the legacy of all women to my music—I wanted my voice, my lyrics, and my music itself to ring with this emerging feminist awakening, through my music. The combination of finding my stride as a working performer and becoming part of a supportive and thriving community of out-and-about lesbians were powerful forces in my development as an artist.

Robin Trower, the creator and producer of the West Coast Women's Music & Cultural Festival, approached me one night after a show and asked if I would be interested in playing. I was honored.

At the time, the festival was held in Yosemite, and it was a bare-breasted, back-to-Mother-Nature extravaganza. I didn't think my music really fit in with the more indie-folk scene—I was more old-school rock and roll—but Robin encouraged me to go.

It became a prolific time for me. I began writing a lot and started testing out original songs when I performed at Vermie's in Pasadena and the Executive Suite in Long Beach. This is the time period when I wrote "Like the Way I Do" and "You Used to Love to Dance." I still love these songs because of the rawness of the feeling and how they captured me at that time in my life.

I was developing a real following. I'll never forget the first night a woman requested one of my songs—"Like the Way I Do." People always got the title wrong—"Like the Way You Do" or "Do It Like Me"—so many varied mashups of titles to that song, which is funny but also understandable. No matter, I was thrilled—they were liking my music!

I also played Que Sera in Long Beach, Robbie's in Pomona, Club Sappho and At My Place in Santa Monica. One Sunday, when I was playing at Vermie's in Pasadena, a few of the regulars from the local women's soccer team came up to me after the show.

"Hey, one of our coaches—Karla Leopold—is married to a guy in the record business—Bill Leopold. Ever hear of him?"

I had.

"Well, Karla says she wants him to come listen to you."

"Really?" I had made a demo tape—not very professional, but it did capture my sound.

The next Sunday Karla came in with the regular group of gals, and apparently she was impressed and told Bill to come see me.

Bill was a character—a talented manager who knew his way

around the music business, and more important, he loved music and musicians. He wasn't just out to make a buck.

A week or so later, Bill shows up at Vermie's—that's when he told me, "You're going to be the next Judy Garland!"

It was my gravelly voice and the intensity of my performances that reminded him of Judy, certainly not the hard life she'd lived.

Bill had managed Bread, Booker T. Jones, and a number of gospel acts that had made records and were doing well. He invited me to lunch at the Copper Penny in Burbank, drove up in a vintage Jaguar XJ, and I admit I was impressed.

Inside, the place was classic old Hollywood—low booths in red leather, each with its own phone.

"Now, it may take one year or it may take five years, but I promise you, I will get you a record deal."

I believed him. But in full disclosure, I really think I signed with him because of that car. I now had a manager. The next thing I did was to call my parents back in Kansas and tell them the news.

And the rest is, as they say, history.

Not that I jumped to immediate stardom—far from it. I was still hustling, playing clubs all around Long Beach and LA, and still doing the West Coast Women's Music & Cultural Festivals, where I met and fell hard for Kathleen. She was one of a long list of women who semi-tortured me. Kathleen was open and honest, caring and sexy, and a total knockout. The only problem? She was not into monogamy at all. I really liked Kathleen, but I couldn't handle feeling so insecure about who else she might be sleeping with.

Later, I would have my share of dating more than one woman at a time, but when I was with Kathleen, I wanted her to be all mine.

That's where my song "Bring Me Some Water" comes from—me trying to be flexible but getting incredibly overwrought and jealous.

Tonight I feel so weak
But all in love is fair
I turn the other cheek
And I feel the slap and the sting of the foul night air
And I know you're only human
And I haven't got talking room
But tonight while I'm making excuses
Some other woman is making love to you
Somebody bring me some water
Can't you see I'm burning alive?
Can't you see my baby's got another lover?
I don't know how I'm gonna survive
Somebody bring me some water
Can't you see it's out of control?
Baby's got my heart and my baby's got my mind
But tonight the sweet devil, the sweet devil's got my soul
Will this aching pass?
Will this night be through?
I wanna hear the breaking glass
I only feel the steel of the red hot truth
And I'd do anything to get it out of my mind
I need some insanity, that temporary kind
Tell me how will I ever be the same?
When I know that that woman is whispering your name
Somebody bring me some water
Can't you see I'm burning alive?

Can't you see my baby's got another lover?
And I don't know how I'm gonna survive
Somebody bring me some water
Can't you see it's out of control?
Baby's got my heart and my baby's got my mind
But tonight the sweet devil, the sweet devil's got my soul
Got my soul
Uh, yeah
Somebody bring me some water
Can't you see I'm burning alive?
Can't you see my baby's got another lover
And I don't know how I'm gonna survive
Somebody bring me some water
Can't you see it's out of control?
Baby's got my heart and my baby's got my mind
But tonight the sweet devil, the sweet devil's got my soul
Baby's got my heart and my baby's got my mind
But tonight the sweet devil, the sweet devil's got my soul

And that's how I felt: Would I survive loving someone so much, knowing she was not really mine?

This framing of love is so unfamiliar to me now. If I'm honest, in my twenties, I didn't understand Kathleen's choice to be non-monogamous; I pretended to, of course. But underneath I had not yet parsed how loving someone so deeply meant not possessing. I see now that love is always a form of surrender, that the very act of loving comes with risk and an essential vulnerability.

*   *   *

Life was hard-charging ahead and I was working my ass off. I thought: *Once I get a record deal and become famous—will Kathleen be able to turn me down then?* I was still looking for that blanket of acceptance and unconditional love, though it was proving to be ever elusive. The only thing I could control was work, which, attached to my ambition to make it as a rock star, gave me a focus that became bigger and badder.

Once Bill took me on, all I could think of was getting a record deal. He took me into the studio and I started to record some demos. This was a new experience for me. My training as a musician was honed at live gigs, where I'd test out the songs. Audience feedback and the acoustics of a live performance were key to how I developed the nuances of the lyrics and music. Sometimes I changed the lyrics or the breaks, depending on how it all felt in the moment. But in the studio, with me and me alone, I had no feedback. The sound felt sterile, even echoey. But Bill was serious.

"Okay, now I want you to record everything you've written."

That was about twenty songs. I was super excited because I was finally recording my own work—not singing anyone else's.

But I did not like my demos at all—actually, I thought they were pretty horrible.

That was in 1983.

To this day, it's hard to re-create what I do live in a recording session. Having someone listening brings the songs alive for me. For many years, I brought friends into the studio so I'd have someone to sing to.

Bill secured for me a publishing deal with Almo/Irving Music, a branch of A&M records. It was not a recording contract, but it was a professional nod to my ability—and it made me feel good to be a working artist. I have always loved writing songs, and this felt no different—except I was writing songs for other people and getting paid for it.

I mostly wrote songs for films, not individual artists. A couple of my songs turned up in movies like *Scenes from the Goldmine*, a really bad movie about the record industry in the '80s. But one thing led to another, and a few years later, the director, Mark Rocco, used almost my entire second album as soundtrack of the film *Where the Day Takes You*, featuring a very young Will Smith.

The publishing gig paid fifty bucks a week, and I had my own office on La Brea, near the Henson studio, which used to be Charlie Chaplin's soundstage. A&M Records was across the street in a beautiful Art Deco building—a stone's throw. I loved going to the office, which had a piano that I could work from.

Kathleen and I were living together in Hollywood, on Mansfield, off of Melrose. When we were together, we were totally together. The sex and emotional intimacy were tender. Being with her made me understand what a real relationship with a woman could be like. But if I went on tour, or she decided to go to a music festival, I would feel incredibly insecure and try to talk myself out of wanting her, loving her. A couple of times, I distracted myself by hooking up with a woman I would meet at one of my gigs. But I was too in love with Kathleen to let anything be more than a one-night stand.

So I did what I did best: I worked.

Each day, I worked on songs from nine to four p.m. and then performed at night at clubs around LA and Long Beach, the same clubs where I'd been building up a following—Vermie's, Executive Suite, At My Place. I played at least five nights a week. I was afraid that if I didn't show up, I'd be forgotten and replaced. One night I was so ill,

I could barely speak, never mind sing. To this day, I can remember the dread of having to make that phone call, telling the manager that I had to cancel my show.

Without a record deal, I had to keep things lively. At one point, I decided to go on a solo tour. I asked Kathleen to come with me, along with another friend, and we mapped out a tour itinerary, focused on women's bars in the southwest and Midwest. Familiar territory from when I visited my grandparents in Arkansas and my road trip with my dad. I ended up playing at the Blue Light—the bar I had visited back in 1982, on my way west to LA from Kansas. (And did Dawn remember me? That would be a no.)

As we drove, I would write—in fact I wrote "You Sleep While I Drive" on that first tour in 1986.

Come on, baby, let's get out of this town
I got a full tank of gas with the top rolled down
There's a chill in my bones
I don't want to be left alone
So baby, you can sleep while I drive
I'll pack my bag and load up my guitar
In my pocket I'll carry my harp
I got some money I saved
Enough to get underway
And baby, you can sleep while I drive
We'll go through Tucson up to Santa Fe
And Barbara in Nashville says we're welcome to stay
I'll buy you glasses in Texas, a hat from New Orleans
And in the morning you can tell me your dreams
You know I've seen it before

This mist that covers your eyes
You've been looking for something
That's not in your life
My intentions are true
Won't you take me with you
And baby, you can sleep while I drive
Oh, is it other arms you want to hold you
The stranger
But lover you're free
Can't you get that with me
Come on, baby, let's get out of this town
I got a full tank of gas with the top rolled down
If you won't take me with you
I'll go before night is through
And baby, you can sleep while I drive

I loved being on the road. There was a rhythm that I'd get into that was both soothing and energizing. The combo of being untethered from "real life," and living simply–with just what we could fit in my car–freed me up to be more creative.

To this day, being on tour has that effect on me.

Finally I got a record deal.

One night I was playing at Que Sera in Long Beach and in comes this producer from A&M Records, and with him was Chris Blackwell, the famous British record producer and founder of Island Records. I knew that he had made a lot of careers, including Bob Marley, Jethro Tull, Cat Stevens, Emerson Lake & Palmer, and U2, to name a few. When he chose to sign me, I could barely see straight I was so excited.

It ended up taking more than two years for me to finish that first record—*Melissa Etheridge*. The first go-round was an overproduced mix of songs that didn't capture me or my sound. I didn't like it, and neither did Chris, who flat-out rejected it. But when I went back to my roots and figured out how to imagine playing for an audience during the recording, the songs came alive, the way they were meant to be.

I think of those early years in Long Beach and LA as some of the last times I felt really free and unencumbered. At that time, freedom meant believing that I didn't have to answer to anyone. Before the record deal, the industry oversight, it was just me making my way. I wasn't yet well-known or famous. I was young. I was naive. I was ambitious and driven to make a name for myself. These are all part of my context at the time, which helps me understand this period of my life and what was working… and what wasn't. Like many twenty-year-olds, I was self-involved and not really mature enough to know how to nurture a relationship. But I wasn't as free as I wanted to believe.

I was preoccupied with making my dream come true, too busy to pay attention to some of the undercurrents within myself. For example, my relationship with Kathleen. I knew she couldn't give me what I wanted, but I stayed in the relationship anyway. I would go on tour to seek relief from the anguish of her nonmonogamy. I worked hard to block out the deeper self-doubt and discomfort. I knew I was desperate for her to commit to me, to have her want me and no one else—but I wasn't listening to what that desperation was really telling me: that I wasn't enough as I am. I was going into my music to process the mixed-up emotions and the angst, but I wasn't really touching it. Deep down, I was afraid of what this meant:

Would I ever be enough for one person? Maybe she sensed something I was hiding that kept her from truly loving me? These were the scary whispers I'd hear in my head when the lights were out and everyone was asleep except for me. Then I'd wake up, put on my smile and that gruff in my voice, and pretend there was no soft side to me, no hidden ghosts inside.

I kept focused on all the hopes and dreams now tied to the record deal. I didn't know what to do with all the feelings—so I just worked and worked and worked and hoped they'd go away. But wounds don't just go away. They didn't mend on their own just because I ignored them. The cover-up would not hold. Something was bound to remind me that there were wounds that still needed healing.

And that's precisely when I met Julie Cypher, the woman I would be involved with for over ten years.

CHAPTER 5

SOMEONE BRING ME SOME WATER

I was twenty-eight years old when Chris Blackwell took me under his wing. He oversaw my musical direction, and a few different producers at Island Records helped me with my first and second albums. I was riding high, feeling myself coming closer and closer to that dream of fame and fortune.

Chris arranged for me to do a music video. In 1988, music videos were *it*! We were filming "Bring Me Some Water," a song that was fast becoming a hit. The producers decided to set up the video shoot at a bar in St. Louis, which was the next stop on tour. I'd already played Minneapolis and Kansas City and was totally psyched to be on my first legit tour. We wanted to capture a live concert feel for the video and I was picturing it in my mind—totally letting loose and jamming to a live audience. My happy place. It was the perfect antidote to the detachment that I experienced when recording in a studio.

I had just gotten my hair and makeup done professionally, which was all very new to me. I'd done my share of fixing myself up when

I went on tour and played at clubs in and around LA—but this was hair and makeup for real! I felt glamorous—like I really was on the road to fame.

When I got on set to film the music video, I tried to brush off my nervousness, telling myself that of course the director would give me a few chances to get it right—being filmed was not something I was used to. I took in the lights, the marks on the floor, and the director's camera and went back to my bus.

When they were ready to start filming, I got off the bus. As I stepped into the street, this dark-haired, exceptionally beautiful woman approached me and introduced herself as the assistant director on the video team.

"Hey, I'm Julie—nice to meet you." She had a side smile and a mischievous glint in her eye, and to me she was just plain hot.

I did not yet know that Julie was married to the actor Lou Diamond Phillips, who at that point was a Hollywood heartthrob, but I'd soon find out that Julie was part of a very cool couple.

But, husband or no husband, Julie was flirting.

So began a relationship that would teach me a lot about myself, and I'd venture to say that as I look back on it, I keep learning from it. Without it, I would never be able to see and embrace how far I've come from that person who dove headfirst into a kind of love addiction.

It took a couple of years for our flirtations to turn into a (more or less) committed relationship. We waited until she had ended her marriage to Lou. For those intervening months, I was crazy busy, touring and playing gigs before, during, and after my first and then my second album was released. I had received my first Grammy nomination for "Bring Me Some Water" and now I was going to be part of this new MTV wave, reaching audiences not just on albums and on tour—but on television. I was as excited as everyone else in rock and roll.

I started writing songs about and for Julie. Desire and longing, laced with confusion and mixed emotions. Add just a little bit of torture: "Let Me Go," "I Want to Come Over," "I'm the Only One"—those were all about Julie.

But I'm getting ahead of myself.

By 1990, Julie and I were living together in a cool house in West Hollywood. Our house had that classic California indoor-outdoor living space with a kidney-shaped pool and comfortable lounge chairs, and soon enough our home became party central.

We were hanging out with other actors and musicians—Brad Pitt, Jennifer Aniston, Dermot Mulroney, and Catherine Keener, all of whom were on the rise. It was all intoxicating for a nobody from Kansas to find herself among these bright lights of the entertainment scene.

I was working on my second album, *Brave and Crazy*, and touring a lot, which I loved.

By this time in the early '90s there was an increase in gay and lesbian activism. Not officially out of the closet, Julie and I were connected to a lot of people who were politically active. I'd met the comedian Kate Clinton at one of the West Coast Women's Music & Cultural Festivals, and Kate introduced me to her partner, Urvashi Vaid, who was then executive director of the National Gay and Lesbian Task Force. Urvashi was working to convince high-profile gays and lesbians (mostly in Hollywood) to come out. Hollywood, for all its show of support for causes, remained stubbornly and fearfully stuck in the closet. Urvashi was one of the first in the movement to connect economics to social standing and politics. She knew then what is so clear now: that without money, people in high places are less likely to care what you have to say. As maddening as that is, by bringing that fact into the open, Urvashi was able to gain some leverage to make real changes.

Alongside Urvashi's work was ACT UP, an international grassroots coalition whose mission was to improve the lives of people suffering from AIDS by advancing medical research and improving treatment. Political momentum and pressure were building.

And though AIDS was first diagnosed in 1981, it wasn't until the 1990s when America started paying attention, and a lot of that awareness finally came from gay pioneers within the entertainment industry. Elton John's 1992 song "The Last Song" was released a year after Freddie Mercury of Queen had died of AIDS. In 1993 the film *Philadelphia* starring Tom Hanks and Denzel Washington garnered significant attention—not only because it was the first feature film to show a man dying of AIDS but also because neither star actor was gay, sending a message: *let's tear down the wall of separation between gay and straight* (the spectrum of LGBTQIA+ not yet having been established). Also released in 1993 was the award-winning made-for-television movie *And the Band Played On*, which was based on the nonfiction book of the same name, capturing the searing story of how a young epidemiologist, Dr. Don Francis, began to investigate the outbreak of a disease that seemed to affect primarily gay men.

I can't say that I've ever considered myself a political activist, but I've always tried to motivate people to pay attention to things that matter. I wanted to show up and do my part, so I helped where

I could and played at a lot of benefits for LGBTQIA+ rights. Like many other musicians who wanted to raise money for AIDS research, I became part of the Red Hot organization, which brought awareness and funding to AIDS-related organizations. For its Red Hot + Latin album *Silencio=Muerte*, I sang "Sin Tener a Dónde Ir (Nowhere to Go)." I am grateful to have been part of this movement, which continues to need support.

*   *   *

For all of the sizzle of our coupledom, Julie and I were far from solid. We had a tempestuous push-pull dynamic. We'd expect too much from each other and hold each other too close. We'd get claustrophobic, and then we would push each other away. Julie would say we needed space. My space came going on tour and hiding in my music. Her space seemed to come from having affairs, with both women and men.

We were drawn to each other in an electric sort of way—but that electricity sometimes caused fires.

When we were together, I tried to satisfy her needs: her need for attention, her need for me, her need for things. It felt like a bottomless well that I couldn't fill. Not that I was aware of it at the time. And right before I could explode, I'd go on tour to recalibrate. I'd hear myself again, find my inner balance, recover from the onslaught of the conflicts between us.

I'd like to say there were enough high points to make up for the friction and the fighting, but this was more or less our scene for most of our time together. I was caught in a cycle of trying to save Julie—from herself, her bad habits, her drinking, her seeming unquenchable need for more. I don't blame her. I see now that I was the one who thought she needed saving by being and doing everything for her. She wasn't asking to be saved. I had assigned that task to myself. Often I'd be confused, hurt, and angry all at once—not understanding my part in the problem.

I believed I wanted to fix Julie and take away her ups and downs, but clearly I was working out something that I couldn't quite pinpoint. Was I reliving the drama and trauma from growing up with my volatile sister? Was I trying to feel empowered to make a difference in Julie's life in a way I couldn't as a child for my mother? I was not holding my own boundaries—I didn't even know what boundaries were. I didn't say to her, *You don't get to hurt me—you don't get to treat me like that.* I lost sight of myself. By focusing on what was wrong with Julie, I did not see that I was lost myself and terribly unhappy. I could not blame Julie for that. I could not save Julie, and Julie did not have the power to make me happy. My own happiness had to come from me. I just didn't know that yet.

There were some high points. We were asked to go to President Bill Clinton's first inauguration in January 1993 and to the very first gay and lesbian Triangle Ball held at the National Press Club. Although Bill and Hillary were gay-friendly, most of the country was still very conservative and ignorant about LGBTQIA+ issues. For those of us in the community, the AIDS crisis was definitely not in the rearview mirror. We all knew too many people who had lost their lives to that horrible disease. We were lucky to have outspoken advocates like Urvashi and Andrew Sullivan and the many others who helped bring to the public's attention so many of these issues.

In his inaugural address, Clinton spoke about how we all had to come together to do something about the world AIDS crisis. Julie and I had been working on the Clinton campaign, and to raise attention and money for a deadly disease that had decimated the gay community.

Julie and I were proud and excited to be included on the stage before the first-ever openly gay event at a presidential inauguration. We gathered along with friends–Kate Clinton and Urvashi Vaid, k.d. lang, Janis Ian, and others. There was no set plan, which meant we were not sure of whether we were expected to speak, sing, or otherwise perform. The cameras were clicking away, and the crowd was buzzing after Joseph Steffan, who had been forced to resign from the US Naval Academy in 1987 for being gay, sang "The Battle Hymn of the Republic." Kate Clinton had called out Tipper Gore, whose wave seemed to lack luster, by saying, "Can one of you queens get over there fast and help Tipper learn how to wave?"

Then when someone handed me a microphone, I leaned into the mic and said, "I'm proud to say I've been a lesbian all my life."

That moment is forever crystallized in my brain. Most people in my orbit knew I was gay, but putting it out there on such a public stage was a whole other level of stepping into myself.

I'd like to say that it was my plan all along to push back against the unspoken but highly condoned *don't ask, don't tell* policy at my record company, but my motivation was not so intentional. I will say that once I was on the other side of my big public reveal, I felt an amazing release. No more hiding behind songs, no more need to keep lyrics gender-neutral.

I had crossed over. Being part of tearing down cultural taboos and stigmas associated with being queer was a powerful experience. I realized how powerful it felt to be part of the tearing down of cultural taboos and stigmas associated with being queer. As Kate

Clinton said near the end of the evening, "We're here, we're queer, and now we're not leaving for a really long time."

When Dan Rather interviewed me soon after, I told him, "It was very empowering. And when we found that we could make a difference in our American government, in politics, it was enlightening."

My friend and fellow musician Janis Ian also came out that night. She was more or less talked into it by the leader of the Human Rights Campaign, Tim McFeeley, a Harvard Law School graduate. At that time HRC had twenty-five thousand members; ten years later, membership was over five hundred thousand.

That next September, I named my new album *Yes I Am*, which sold six million copies in America. I was blown away when I was nominated and won another Grammy for "Come to My Window," still one of my most requested songs when I tour, along with "I'm the Only One" and "If I Wanted To."

Before this time, I had become used to living a gay life under the radar, but society had begun to change–k.d. lang was out; Elton John was out; a few other entertainers were beginning to consider coming out. But it was all pretty novel at the time, and the money people in Hollywood and the music industry were still very conservative, often stoking fears and threatening the loss of careers. I was not unaware of the possible ramifications of coming out, but I simply felt it was time to let myself be seen for who I really am–a gay woman who is also a singer-songwriter.

Sadly, we would all be disappointed when, a few years later, in 1996, Clinton passed the Defense of Marriage Act (DOMA). It felt like all of our support during his campaign with Al Gore was a waste, or more accurately, a betrayal of our trust in him. Even so, being part of the Triangle Ball and onstage inauguration night became a victory to celebrate, and I remain grateful for having been a small part of it.

From that time, I forged a relationship with Al Gore, something that would come to mean a lot to me in a few more years.

*   *   *

In 1996, as I was about to go on tour for *Your Little Secret*, my fifth album, Julie declared that she wanted to have a baby. Given the issues with our relationship, this might not have been the most sound consideration, but babies bring blessings, and I was hopeful about it and went all in with starting a family. I remember thinking to myself, *Maybe having a child would make us both happier—with each other and for each other*. I wanted to trust in the idea that new life would bring us love.

I had never imagined becoming a parent, never mind carrying a child. That just wasn't part of my biological imperative. But Julie was ready for it and got pregnant quickly. Our non-anonymous sperm donor was the late David Crosby, which was a fact not widely known when Julie got pregnant.

I was on tour in Europe for most of Julie's pregnancy. I had two big hits on that album—"I Want to Come Over" and "Nowhere to Go." I felt terrible being away while Julie was pregnant—and have often wondered if that triggered the ultimate end of that relationship. Looking back, I can see now how my absence at the time was a giant, flashing red arrow that signaled the disconnect—physical, mental, emotional—in our relationship.

The pregnancy raised questions on both sides: Julie was questioning whether she "was really gay," and I was questioning her commitment to our relationship and became worried about her stepping out with a man.

I was reminded of how Kathleen could not and did not want to be monogamous. Now Julie, the woman with whom I was going to share a family, was questioning her sexuality. I told myself that she was just being dramatic and trying to get a rise out of me. Maybe she was resentful that I was on the road and not with her; being pregnant and alone, I assumed she felt vulnerable—a potent feeling. There were other moments when I thought Julie preferred men, and I'd feel a hole in the pit in my stomach, a familiar dread: I am not enough. I will never be enough. I would have paranoid fantasies about what she was really up to when I was on the road. I also felt guilty for not being there for Julie, and that should have informed any speculations I was making about what Julie may or may not have been up to in my absence. I may not have trusted Julie, but I also did not trust myself.

As I toured Europe, I often found myself questioning whether or not having this baby would be our salvation or do us in. In hotel after hotel across Europe, I dreamed and hoped that I had what it took to be a good mom, a good partner, a good lover. I can't even say I knew what those qualities were, exactly.

But I was playing one song that always reminded me of what was out of harmony with Julie and me.

I WANT TO COME OVER

I know you're home
You left your light on

You know I'm here
The night is thin
I know you're alone
I watched the car leave
Your lover is gone
Let me in
Open your back door
I just need to touch you once more
I want to come over
To hell with the consequence
You told me you loved me
That's all I believe
I want to come over
It's a need I can't explain
To see you again
I want to come over
I know your friend
You told her about me
She filled you with fear
Some kind of sin
How can you turn
Denying the fire
Lover I burn
Let me in
Open your back door
I just need to touch you once more
Oh, oh
I want to come over
To hell with the consequence

You told me you loved me
That's all I believe
I want to come over
It's a need I can't explain
To see you again
I want to come over

I used to think that song was solely about unbridled desire, but between the lines, and in the way I got into it when I sang it full throttle, I know that song is also a desperate plea: I can convince you that I'm worth it if you just let me. The question is who is the "you" I was talking about? I thought it was about Julie, but maybe it was about me—that I was the one shaken and lost.

I got home from touring right before Christmas, and Julie was way ready to have the baby. She'd stopped working months earlier, so she was wound up—bored and anxious in anticipation of all to come.

She was due at the end of January, and by that time, she was getting more and more uncomfortable, and I was becoming more and more anxious. Our friend Laura Dern predicted that the baby would be born on her birthday, February 10—and guess what? In the middle of the night on February 10, 1997, our beautiful Bailey Jean Cypheridge came into this world and into my arms.

Julie always slept in, so the mornings were time for me and Bailey and the BabyBjörn. Her round little face, her big brown eyes, her delightful squeal. We walked and talked—well, I did most of the talking. And singing and cooing and laughing.

I was in love with this darling little girl.

Bailey walked and talked at ten months old. She had this crazy vocabulary even at that age. Once when we were on a plane, I was chatting with another mother whose child was about Bailey's age—we chatted about schedules, sleep, and other new-parent info. There was always something new to discover and share.

Then Bailey, who was sitting in my lap, turns to the plane window and says, "Airplane! Many airplanes!"

The other woman looked at me and then back at Bailey. "She's only ten months old?" I think she thought I got my kid's age wrong!

Bailey wasn't quite a year old yet, and Julie started talking about having another baby, with David Crosby again as the sperm donor. She didn't want Bailey to be an only child. I pushed back a little bit. We were fighting a lot and went into therapy again to sort through all the contradictions of our relationship: we both loved Bailey without question, and we were devoted to our family. But what did the ever-present tension mean? Was it possible to channel our love and devotion and close the gap of disconnection between us?

Whenever Julie brought up her desire to get pregnant again, I pointed out that we were not exactly doing well as a couple. If Bailey hadn't been there, tucked between us, I'm not sure we'd even have had soft words between us.

Despite our disagreements about having another baby, Julie persisted. She had spent months studying her cycle and was very determined to get pregnant. She arranged to meet David Crosby in New York City, and went ahead and got inseminated on her own. And got pregnant.

There was not really a lot I could do at that point. I was distraught and tried to deal with it by talking with my therapist about the situation. Clearly our partnership of making significant decisions together had fallen apart.

We met with the same therapist for both our couple's work and our individual therapy. It was an unconventional setup, but we thought it would make us feel more united.

I remember one individual therapy session when I told the therapist that Julie had gone and gotten pregnant. The therapist, trying not to take sides, looked distraught, which did not quite help me feel better about the continued disconnect between me and Julie.

By the time sweet Beckett was born in November 1998, Julie and I fought more than we loved. After a fight, we would both try and make up, but I honestly didn't know what to say or do to make things right.

COMING AND GOING

We weren't doing much better. Our lives were hectic with two babies. I was stressing about getting back to work, and Julie was drinking. Added to this pressure-cooker situation was the fact that we were leading very public lives. Also we were not married, or rather we could not get married as two women, since DOMA had passed in 1996, and I felt enormous pressure to be a model gay family, knowing, of course, that we weren't.

I had taken almost two years away from touring, and even though I was happy spending more time with the kids, I started to feel that pull of the road—and I had bills to pay.

I made an exception with a trip to Australia during the fall of 1999. Julie and the kids would typically have come on tour with me, but Australia was just too far, and the trip was only going to be for ten days, so I went alone.

When I got back from Australia, I came into the house and went straight to Beckett, who was eleven months old by then. I picked him up and put him in my lap. He turned his beautiful round face away from me, and my heart sank. He wouldn't look me in the eyes. It broke my heart. I know now that Beckett's detachment after not seeing me for a few weeks was normal behavior for an infant, but it tapped into my fear that being away from him was irresponsible. Of course, many parents travel when their kids are young, but I was feeling the fragility of our family situation, and it made me deeply uncomfortable.

Meanwhile, every time I did an interview, I'd be asked who the father of the kids was. The press started to speculate, and the paparazzi started following me and Julie. We were afraid that something would happen to the kids, so we spoke to David Crosby and his wife, Jan, and they gave us their blessing to come out with it.

In the new year, to ring in the new millennium, we posed for the February cover of *Rolling Stone*: Julie, me, Bailey, and Beckett, along with David Crosby and Jan.

By September of that year, Julie and I were over.

*   *   *

The last years with Julie had been exceptionally distraught. Although I had reached my dream of becoming a rock star, proudly come out to the world, won Grammys, and appeared on the covers of *Rolling Stone* and *Newsweek*, I was racked with guilt about the failure of mine and Julie's relationship. My breakthrough album— *Yes I Am*—was a huge success. Overnight, I had become a LGBTQIA+ icon, which also meant that our breakup was very painfully public.

People had opinions—many of them harsh, many of them based on inaccuracies. Ever since our kids were born, I'd felt enormous pressure not only to protect them but also to be a perfect parent, part of a perfect couple. When our relationship fell apart, it seemed that I was letting down the whole gay community. I imagined the wider world would whisper a thousand *I told you so*s and warnings about gay marriage, gay couples having children, gay rights in general.

Deep down, I believed I was a good parent—but a gnawing dread kept after me. I believed I had given my best to a relationship that was complicated and dysfunctional and ultimately made neither of us happy. But in all the misunderstandings, hurt feelings, and general emotional chaos and disarray, I still felt responsible for the pain and havoc surrounding us at the time, as if I alone were responsible for jeopardizing my children's sense of safety and security. As I wrestled with these feelings of failure and confusion about my part in all of it, I sought help by continuing therapy. I turned to other healers. I sorted through my misgivings and soothed myself by writing songs. None of it felt good. I did not feel good about life, myself, my music.

Later, I'd come to realize that my forging ahead with having a family with Julie despite the red flags pointing to the relationship's instability was a further reflection of my wanting to make people happy and my erroneous belief that I could. I know now that the only person I can make happy is myself; all I can do for another, including Julie, is love.

But then, at one of the highest points in my musical career, I was not happy. Life was all struggle, a state of being that now I know means I was not in sync with Spirit. The lows felt overwhelming and debilitating at times, like permanent dead ends rather than pauses along a path.

When I wrote the album *Breakdown*, I was in the eye of the hurricane with Julie. I was dieting and working out like a fiendish robot. My trainer at the time would say, "No dinner makes you thinner." I had lost a sense of connection to my body, which reflected so much about what was wrong with not only my relationship with Julie, who pressured me to look a certain way, but more important, in my relationship with myself. Julie had always wanted me to be thinner, more fit, sexier—the list felt endless. And I fell prey to that pressure. The machine of the music industry didn't help and only reinforced an unrealistic ideal body. I often found myself thinking, *If I could just look a certain way, then everything would be okay.*

After the breakup, I began writing the songs for what would become my album *Skin*. I had gone into the studio with David Cole—just the two of us. I needed to concentrate. I can remember writing "Lover Please" to a shuffle beat. Listening now, all I can think of is how anemic it sounds. There was a plaintive whine—"Please don't go away." Clearly I was still in emotional agony. Then I wrote "The Prison," which was my attempt to keep from complete despair. I couldn't trust myself anymore, which is why the metaphor of living in my own prison resonated. Then with "Walking on Water," I was literally asking for a miracle.

"It's Only Me" was a pivotal point in the album; if you listen closely, you can literally hear me scream. I wanted to capture the visceral sense of pain, confusion, and outrage and the cathartic release of just letting it all go. I wanted to nail the point of change in the album and my life. I had begun to feel like a big change was coming. I wanted to heal. The songs on that album are purposefully arranged for a lift at the end.

IT'S ONLY ME

They say the Lord giveth and the Lord taketh away
Well, it was definitely gone when I woke up today
I walked up to the mirror to see
It's only me
I got out of the kitchen, I couldn't stand the heat
Back into my skin and out on the street
Lookin' for a little salvation
It's only me
Baby, you can just pretend
That maybe you can love again
But babe I know better
It's only me
And wherever you are tonight
The satisfaction you invite
Nobody knows better
It's only me
Well, I went down to the revival
To give my soul a chance
And the DJ spoke to God
And the congregation danced
And I heard a sound and I turned around
It's only me
I found a little angel who had fallen from the sky
And I took that little angel and I taught her how to fly
When the night is done and the morning comes
It's only me
Baby you can just pretend

That maybe you can love again
But babe I know better
It's only me
And wherever you are tonight
The satisfaction you invite
Nobody knows better
It's only me, only me
All you'll ever want
And all you'll ever need
And all you'll ever taste
And all you'll ever bleed
Look deep inside you
It's only me
Baby you can just pretend
That maybe you can love again
But babe I know better
It's only me
And wherever you are tonight
The satisfaction you invite
Nobody knows better
Its only me
Ohâ?¦

Another song I wrote to help me soldier on is "Down to One":

What went right
What went wrong
Doesn't really matter much
When it's gone

Was it too hard to try

Was it too hard to lie

Did you just grow tired of hello and good-bye

Was it the naked truth that made you run

Where do I go now

That I'm down to one

Sooner or later

We all end up walking alone

I'm down to one

My heart is a traitor

It led me down this road

Now it's done

I'm down to one

I want to know where I failed

I want to know where I sinned

'Cause I don't want to ever feel this way again

Was the wanting too deep

Did it block your sun

Where do I go now

That I'm down to one

I guess sooner or later

We all end up walking alone

I'm down to one

My heart is a traitor

It led me down this road

Now it's done

I'm down to one

What am I supposed to think

What am I gonna say

What did I ever know

About this love anyway
Down to one
My heart is a traitor
It led me down this road
And I'm down to one
I guess sooner or later
We all end up walking alone
I'm down to one
My heart is a traitor
And now it's done
Down to one
I'm down to one

Even now when I read these lyrics, and sometimes when I'm up onstage singing them, I can feel how hard it was for me to pull myself back into my center. How much I was searching for a new kind of energy, a fresh start. I wanted lightness and love. I wanted healing and freedom. I wanted laughter and touch and all that sex and sensuality do for us as humans.

Yes—I was starting to believe that hope could return. That my creative energy would once again carry me through. And I wanted desperately to be bright and clear for my two young kids.

What I couldn't quite see at the time, despite all my determination, was how locked I was in old, dysfunctional patterns. I could see the part of myself I wanted to be—the passionate lover, a fervent musician energized and driven by a desire to create, someone filled with the courage and confidence to pursue my dreams, who never shied away from a challenge, even in love. But I was out of position. I didn't really know how to love without fear.

Many of my choices came from a fear-based mentality. This kind of thinking constrained me. I was beginning to see that despite the big, bold dreams I had as a young girl, a lot of my motivation was attached to the fear that I might not make it outside of Leavenworth, that I was making things up, as my mom had told me. For years, I was unaware of how I was unconsciously curtailing my experience of myself and all that I could do and feel. I'd push my feelings into songs, in search of explanations and in hopes of relief. And for a while, the release would come. But it also hurt. Each album, each song, was an attempt to find relief from a pain I couldn't locate inside of me.

Like the songs on *Breakdown* and *Skin*, the lyrics are filled with longing and confusion, a drumbeat of ache and not knowing. And though I still love many of these songs and play them often on tour, I now see how these songs were a dumping ground for all my questions and feelings. Running underneath all of them was this steady stream of fear. I was not living in a place of trust or love. I was trying to escape my discomfort by striving too hard and looking outside of myself for affirmation. Despite the fact that my dreams were indeed coming true, I didn't yet realize the missing piece: it all had to circle back to love. And that to finally vanquish fear you had to choose love.

Ultimately my first taste of loving without expectations and without fear came to me through my children. I had begun to think of my love for my children as a divine contract in which I was going to love them for who they were, seeing them for who they are, accepting them, and offering them unyielding grace and understanding.

Living in Spirit helped me to recognize the patterns of my behaviors for what they really were: cries for help and healing. I started to see how my responses to certain events had become sticky, un-examined ways of thinking and feeling, causing me heartache and unhappiness.

I understand now that I participated in romantic relationships that helped me to keep those barriers to self-knowledge in place. When we have a healthy relationship with ourselves, we are able to find partners who build us up, not tear us down.

Part of this dynamic was my clinging to the belief that if I could make this other person happy, everything will be fine with me. But, of course, we can't *make* anyone else happy. We can be kind and honest and giving and present—to ourselves and to those we love—but whether that makes someone happy is not the point.

I had no way of knowing this when the pattern was established as the child of a distant and depressed mom and the victim of childhood abuse. I unconsciously tried to make myself smaller and smaller so that the other person—my mother, my mentally ill sister, my lover—felt bigger. I know now that this was a way of forfeiting my own desires, which I've come to see, sadly, as common in en-tertainers. We know how to bring joy into the room, we're able to lighten the mood, but not for ourselves. Might it be true that per-formers are bringing it all to an audience to garner that love they missed?

Spirit would teach me sovereignty. Spirit would teach me self-love. Spirit would teach me the healing path.

PART II

THE SEEKING YEARS

CHAPTER 6

NO GOING BACK

After my heroic dose in 2003, I went about my normal daily routines, trying to stay grounded, but I was totally distracted by the episode and hungry to understand what had happened. How could I feel so different in my body and in my mind? What was it about the cannabis that triggered this clarity? This sense that I was connected to the world in a new way? That those connections were both inside and outside of myself?

I started to research and learned that the cannabis had triggered a hallucinogenic experience; it was not a break from reality—it was more like a sensory enhancement coupled with a mind expansion, where thoughts, emotions, and sensations are magnified and more numerous. This was caused, in simplistic terms, by an increase in synaptic communication—basically my nervous system lit up in response to the high dose of cannabis. In some ways, the experience was like a really long orgasm—full of intense pleasure that radiated both inward and outward, giving me an ecstatic sensual awareness. I had always lived in my body in a very physical way, but this quality took on a spiritual dimension.

I have always felt myself close to God. As a young girl when I'd go to Sunday school or sang hymns in the youth choir, I experienced God's presence. At the time, God to me was Jesus, a loving prophet and teacher who taught his followers about kindness and compassion, about treating our fellow beings with love and unconditional acceptance. I have always believed in the essential goodness of people. Something I learned from my dad. I have also always believed in the spirit world, a world that explained phenomena in ways other than "just the facts." When I was in my twenties I went through a past-life regression, and I still regularly get my astrological chart done on my birthday and have my cards read on occasion. I had always been searching the non-dualistic realm, though I couldn't say I'd ever experienced what that might actually feel like. The journey I went on happened, I believe now, because I was ready for it. Assisted, of course, by ingesting *a lot* of cannabis. Now, my understanding of Spirit was broadening, connecting me to a wider understanding of reality. Every wisdom tradition teaches us in some way that we are a part of a larger whole. Among other teachings, Spirit shows us that we, individually, are not the whole story. Once we submit to awe and become aware of the vastness of possibilities, we can connect more deeply with everything and everyone around us. Taking the "I" out of the equation—even if for a blessed moment—makes room for a more spirit-filled existence.

I dove into all I could find on what's behind these ecstatic experiences. I needed to understand. I read newer books on neuroscience and how the brain works; I read books by psychologists and physicists and believed I was being called to explore the world and understand what these seekers have been describing for eons: how to access a higher state of consciousness, a state of enlightenment that offers perhaps a deeper sense of meaning and purpose in our lives. In some ways, this experience made me feel hopeful when contemplating the existential questions of life: What's the meaning of life? Why am I here? Is this all there is?

One important book I discovered at this time was written by philosopher Ken Wilber. In his book *A Brief History of Everything*, Wilber sketches out a new way to conceive of the relationship between humanity and the world. Wilber also points to what we can—and must—learn from the mystical traditions of the world for access to, and knowledge of, a transcendental reality that has always existed—across time periods and cultures. He was making the connections between individuals and the collective in a way that blew my mind but also made so much sense. I really did feel more connected to the world at large and more responsible for how I acted, thought, and felt and how all of those actions impacted others.

One concept that helped me understand how to live in wholeness was the idea of "contrast." Think about the concepts of good vs. evil, dark and light, yin and yang. You can't have one without the other. In the Bible from my childhood, I remembered that the book of Genesis was founded on how creation happened through the transformation of night into day. This does not mean the literal creation of day and night. It means that very early on in creation, contrast and balance were defined and created.

I began to understand that this principle of contrast was a reflection of the property of balance that existed in all aspects of the universe and it pointed to an essential awareness of nonjudgment: any two contrasting energies are neither "good" nor "bad"; they just are.

Think of how our way of functioning in the world depends on contrast: contrasting colors, contrasting sizes, contrasting sensations, contrasting tastes. There was no hot without cold. No silence without noise. And for me, I was beginning to take this to heart: I could not really know happiness if I didn't know sadness. But what was I to do: If our human perception was naturally tied to contrast, and led to a subtle but real unconscious bias many of us are unaware of, how do we get to that place of true awareness of non-duality that promises integration and peace? I think it has something to do with not judging the contrasts—by not valuing light over shadow, silence over noise, good over bad, but rather by accepting what is all without judgment.

Moments from that summer night would come back to me at weird times, remembering having heard voices and feeling like I was getting a type of download straight into my consciousness. As I read about gnostic religions and the connections people like Wilber were making between science and spirituality, I felt guided to start breaking bad habits. I found myself being less compliant and more comfortable standing up for myself. I started to trust my gut.

I also read books by Neale Walsch, Wayne Dyer, and Eckhart Tolle, who believed in the law of attraction, and that we have the power to manifest the life we desire when we manifest from a place of authenticity. They, too, were questioning the implications of limiting ourselves to a binary existence and showing that even though we live in a dualistic world—the light and dark, the good and bad—we can and should experience the wholeness. If you try to block out either side, you lose the power of insight that comes from the unified field.

I began to see that I create the reality that I perceive. That my thoughts and feelings are different expressions of the same energy. And that since we are all, at our core, made up of this energy, I was in charge—I could shape my experience. I was now in charge of my health and my happiness. To paraphrase French philosopher Pierre Teilhard de Chardin, I am a spiritual being having a human experience.

After I delved into religion, physics, and philosophy, I investigated ancient Indigenous cultures and how the shamans and medicine men and women of these cultures had been using sacred plant medicines for thousands of years. Peyote, psilocybin (magic mushrooms), cannabis—plant medicines found in many ancient cultures as methods for healing and convening with the spirit world.

Back when I was still living in Boston and hanging out with some gals at Prelude, a small lesbian bar in the Back Bay, someone asked me if I wanted to try mescaline (a processed form of peyote that has entheogenic and medicinal properties and that was used by Indigenous North Americans). I knew nothing about it at the time. I was a mere nineteen years old and had never even been drunk or high. I said yes to a small purple pill and I remember thinking to myself, *Missy, you are definitely not in Kansas anymore.*

That was my very first journey. Mescaline has a psychoactive effect, meaning it makes you feel high and slightly hallucinogenic. My mind was blown open for a very short time, and then it quickly shut back down. I do have a distinct memory of playing the cigarette machine under the bar speakers like a Hammond organ.

It might be useful to take a moment to talk about some of these substances, especially as we are entering a psychedelic renaissance and people are again studying their possible benefits for healing.

We have been on this road before, in the '70s. But more than fifty years ago, Richard Nixon declared an uninformed and racist "War on Drugs" by getting Congress to pass the Controlled Substances Act. The nonaddictive entheogens were lumped together as Schedule I, along with life-destroying substances like heroin, cocaine, and meth. But the truth is, cannabis, mescaline, psilocybin, and MDMA are all basically nonaddictive and can be used as healing medicines. Nonprohibited substances like cigarettes are responsible for over five hundred thousand deaths per year. Alcohol is responsible for over one hundred thousand deaths per year. And prescribed pharmaceuticals cause more than two hundred fifty thousand deaths a year. We have a lot to learn about what helps us and what harms us. My own journeys have been profoundly affecting.

Inspired by reading across disciplines to further educate myself, I also returned to some of my favorite poets—Maya Angelou, Carolyn Forche, and Mary Oliver. They all seemed to understand that there is more to reality than meets the eye. Poetry has the power to launch an alternate state of mind in a different way than the effects of entheogens, but powerful nonetheless.

The work of Barbara Hand Clow, the spiritualist and astrologer, introduced me to a whole new level of understanding of metaphysics and cosmology, especially in her novel *The Pleiadian Agenda*. I was fascinated by the idea that we as human beings are typically unaware of the multiple realities of the universe. But if we work at it, we can learn to access different dimensions, especially the energetic realm beyond physical sight. I was suddenly hungry to understand this other plane of our existence.

The most influential book I read, one that taught me how to love and practice love and live a life of Spirit, was *The Four Agreements* by the spiritual teacher Don Miguel Ruiz. A short but powerful book, it essentially asks us to reexamine how we think about ourselves in relation to our *self*, our person, others, and the world. When I discovered this book, I felt it was written just for me.

The very first time I read it, I had to sit and reread the pages to fully comprehend all that he was saying. But as I returned to it again and again over the years, I saw that it was so simple. He speaks about the power of our attention to shape our experience. How what we choose to pay attention to really matters. If I wake up worried about X, the day will be drawn to that and I will stay in a narrow, contracted frame of mind. If instead I choose to focus on Y, my energy expands. This does not mean I deny or ignore the challenges in my life, more that I put out into the universe that which I want in return—another form of the law of attraction. We create what we want to see, and what we see is what we put forth.

Ruiz also speaks about how easy it is to absorb the beliefs of others without realizing what we're doing. This was true of my relationships—first with Julie and later with Tammy. I took on their points of view, the view of the world through their lens of struggles. I didn't know then that I had a choice, and that my view, my lens, was right there all along. The same was true when I looked back at my relationship with my mother. I now can see how a lot of my rebelling against her, my resenting her coldness, her distance, was my way of trying to not be like her, and yet she was still in my head, holding me back for so many of my twenties and even into my thirties. That wasn't her fault.

Ruiz also speaks about the fear of rejection and how judging ourselves and others is the root cause of pain and unhappiness, because it creates a victim mentality that holds us back from love and truth. He says the key to living a life anchored by love is simple if you make four agreements with yourself:

To be impeccable with your word. Notice what you say even to yourself and be as truthful as you can so you can know exactly what's inside of you. Use words with care.

Don't take anything personally. This agreement asks us to see ourselves as separate from how others may see us or what they may think and say–about us or anyone else. It's our responsibility to maintain our own sovereignty, to listen to ourselves and keep our boundaries clear. This stance suggests a path of nonjudgment–of ourselves and others.

Don't make assumptions. This agreement backs up the second one. It's about our tendency to assume that we know what people are saying or doing; we can never know another person in this way. Often, we really don't realize how much energy we use, trying to figure out what people are thinking, and then get caught in an outward-facing, other-focused mentality. Nine times out of ten any conclusion we draw about another person's motivation or reasons behind their behavior is way off, and we've created a nontruth. Staying in our mindset means not jumping to conclusions about how or why others act the way they do; it asks us to listen, truly listen.

The fourth agreement is amazingly simple: *just do your best*, always. My motto for sure. Then you are sure that you are not taking things personally; if in every moment you can meaningfully and honestly say to yourself, *I am doing my best*, then you know you are being truthful and true to yourself.

I try to practice Ruiz's spiritual code of conduct every day. When I wake up I remind myself I am grateful to be alive and for all that I have to give and offer. I admit, it isn't always easy.

Back to the time of that first profound journey, when I was living with Tammy and enjoying all the lightness and fun we had together, but now there was something else I couldn't let go of. This opening and the subsequent reading and studying I was doing still didn't help me to fully grasp what these mystics and poets had access to that I didn't. Was this the concept of everlasting life? Paradise with the almighty? The ultimate end to the feeling of separation that comes with an earthly existence? I was sensing that the answers to these questions were on my horizon and that soon Spirit would show me, through my choosing love, that I was not, after all, separate, but connected.

*   *   *

The anchors at this time in my life were my two loves: Bailey, who was four years old, and Beckett, about to turn three. These two were my heart. My life as a mother was like a divine contract—I had a clear belief that my job was to help them become the people they were meant to be. I didn't want to assert any expectations—just because Bailey loved to read, didn't mean she was going to become an English professor.

I had a strong sense I only had so much time with these little beings before they would be out in the world and on their own, charting their own lives. I was also supremely aware of wanting to have healthy relationships with Bailey and Beckett—to never lie, to never pretend, to always be fair and direct with them. I didn't want my complicated relationships with my own parents, my crazy-ass sister, the lovers from my past, to touch my precious kids. It had become clear that so many of my old relationships were transactional in order to earn their love and their loyalty. But now my

understanding of myself in relation to others had shifted drasti-
cally. I could no longer play the role of someone who promises to
deliver them happiness. That is not my job, and my efforts to do so
came from a place of dishonesty in myself as I suppressed my own
feelings in a futile effort to make another happy. It doesn't work,
and absolutely no one benefits from that behavior.

For the most part, I kept these thoughts to myself as I tried to
walk a bit differently through the world. I continued to read about
how Indigenous cultures didn't just believe in the nonmaterial
world, they connected to it daily; it wasn't just part of their mythol-
ogy, their story of creation and life, it was a dimension of their lived
experience. I didn't know how any of this would translate into my
role as a mother, but I held close this new way of being and tried to
be as present as possible with my kids.

At the time of the heroic dose, we all lived in a house in Mandeville Canyon, near Brentwood. The kids would go back and forth
between the home I shared with Tammy and Julie's house. Tammy
was great with Beckett and Bailey. She was warm and friendly and
seemed to love when they came to stay with us. She'd get down
and play on the floor with them. She helped toilet train Beckett.
Together we took them on mini hikes near our house. We all ate
together. Tammy helped me get them to bed at night, never an
easy task. It was becoming very clear to me that Tammy wanted to
have her own kids one day.

As I began to lean into the energy of Spirit in my life, as I woke
into love as my living mantra, I was learning that I could no longer keep up the fortress that I had erected within me. These walls
had kept me from feeling hurt and from accessing the pain points.
I was realizing that if you build a wall inside, you also keep out

deep joy. We don't get to feel only the good stuff. Feeling deep joy and love means to also invite those feelings we most often try to avoid: sadness, anger, shame, resentment. Meaning, by keeping those walls around my heart, I realized I wasn't fully accessing the love inside of me. We don't get to parse which feelings we have—we either shut them all down or invite them all in. We can't have one side without the other. So over the past few years, I've been tearing down these walls to invite it all in. I won't say it isn't scary as hell sometimes.

CHAPTER 7

A MESSAGE FROM ABOVE

The trigger to my big change felt sudden, but in reality, the transformation that marked a very real before and after in my life happened gradually. There were spontaneous moments of insight but also very concrete pitfalls, backslides, and challenges.

For a number of years in my thirties, I was dealing with some physical ailments that interfered with my ability to act as if everything was okay. I had developed an annoying and painful case of cystic acne, not great for someone who worked in the public eye. It was my body's way of telling me that all was not well. An overload of stress at the time was contributing to my sense of unease, and my body was in revolt: the breakup with Julie, the house moves, trying to keep my career going strong. Balance was not part of my life. To make matters worse, the doctor who prescribed Accutane, a strong antibiotic to combat the acne, didn't tell me about its side effects.

During the summer of 2001, Tammy and I had been invited to stay with my friend Steven Spielberg and his wife out in the Hamptons. The trip also coincided with publicity events for my first book.

I was not feeling good about talking about the book. I did not want to be questioned about the breakup with Julie, and I was worried about interviewers wanting to drag my kids into the story. My mom was telling me that I shouldn't have said anything about my sister being abusive. I was feeling very uncomfortable and exposed but didn't have a plan for how to deal with it. I was very, very stressed.

On the plane heading east, I started to feel sick to my stomach, light-headed and weak. By the time we got to the Spielbergs' house, I was doubled over in pain and Steven decided to call an ambulance. I was rushed to the emergency room at the local hospital, where the ER physician immediately ran tests, but told me he thought I was probably having an acute allergic reaction to something I ate.

Not the case.

In those early days with Tammy, I had just let it all go. We ate whatever we wanted—takeout, fried food, Pop-Tarts, and more! I ate everything I had denied myself during the years with Julie, and eating like shit felt like a wicked release. Until it didn't.

I'd suffered from GI issues in the past, but until I landed in the hospital and the doctors told me my whole gut was out of whack, I hadn't really taken my stomach trouble seriously.

It was a summer weekend, but Southampton Hospital was quiet. To be safe, they put me in a private room so I wouldn't be bothered by anyone hunting for sick celebrities.

Around midnight, the hospital suddenly became super busy. A nurse moved me to an interior room on a floor that felt dark and empty—I had the feeling that I was the only one there.

I sensed the commotion from the other parts of the hospital. It turned out that a young woman had run her car into a crowded nightclub, injuring sixteen people.

When the doctors returned with my test results, they explained that I had a very bad case of C. difficile. Typically, this bacterial infection affects older people or those with compromised immune systems. Why did I get C. diff? Because the Accutane had destroyed the good bacteria in my gut and now it was overrun by so much bad bacteria that my body could not fight it. I was massively dehydrated, and my immune system was unable to handle a fast-spreading infection. I was forced to stay in the hospital for three nights, until I was stabilized and sent back to the Spielbergs'.

Needless to say, that trip was a mini-disaster, and I couldn't wait to get back to California. After a few weeks, I recovered, but that episode reminded me that I couldn't take my health for granted. Looking back at how and why I got so perilously sick, I realize that I had not been treating my body with care and reverence. I'd put myself out of balance and jeopardized my health.

At the same time, pressure was mounting on me professionally because I was not in sync with myself. I felt anxious about how to bring the experience of my spiritual awakening into my music. I'd been working on a new album, *Lucky*, which was all about love, lust, and sex. I was having a blast in my new relationship with Tammy, discovering some of what I'd been really needing and wanting in my life. A welcome playfulness, now that I was on the other side of my difficult relationship with Julie. The album was an attempt to reconnect with my creativity, recenter my bearings, and to explore these new feelings. Even the name of the album—*Lucky*—was a declaration of celebration. But there was a disconnect. On the one hand, I really did feel like celebrating. I was hopeful about the future and excited to be free from all that ending things with Julie had entailed—the meetings with lawyers, the therapy sessions, the settlement money, the angry calls, the disagreements about what was best for Bailey and Beckett. Julie was a fighter, and I abhorred arguing. I was forced to confront all of the painful things between us in the most strenuous circumstances. I longed for an amicable breakup, but that takes both sides with the same aspiration.

To complicate matters further, the music industry was going through a significant change during the early aughts. Music was turning super poppy—artists like NSYNC, Britney Spears, and Christina Aguilera were at the top of the charts. None of the radio stations would even play rock and roll anymore. *American Idol* was huge. Music videos were on their way out. At the same time, the internet had changed the way people could listen to and access music. The old business model had shifted to streaming—like a lot of where media was headed—but it hadn't settled into a model anyone could rely on. It was an unsettling time in the music biz. I remember going to my record company's main headquarters in a big glossy building on the edge of Hollywood. Two years before, the company occupied much of the building with many floors devoted to producers, talent, etc. Now only three or four floors were occupied.

A lot of musicians were feeling the fallout. Grunge was suddenly out of fashion. The great bands Pearl Jam and Nirvana were suddenly off the radar, playing around with tech, rock and roll, and basically trying to create their own sound. Some rock musicians went country. It was as if everyone was running away from rock and roll.

In response to the times, my producers were pressuring me to record covers. I loved performing great cover songs—I had visceral attachments to many artists that came before me, and singing their songs had always been a form of connection. But recording a cover for my album? That was a backslide for my career, and it felt like a slap in the face. Was I really losing my momentum as an artist?

So as I was trying to live in Spirit, a state of being that I still didn't quite grasp because it was not so much a feeling as a calling to shift my soul. And everything around me was shifting as well. In hindsight, I realize how this deep discomfort with change and the deep yearning I felt were all part of the same thing. The world does not coalesce around your awakening to light the path with ease and a promise of not faltering. Your awakening helps you to walk in a chaotic world.

Still, as I looked around at my peers at the time, I shook my head and wondered how I fit in. I tried to keep my chin up and find a way through music—which is what I've always done. But the path was anything but clear.

Lucky was an effort to move away from that chrome-plated heart to a soft, open heart, but still hold true to my rock-and-roll soul. I was singing about Tammy in "Come on Out Tonight," wondering if she really knew what she was in for when it came to living in the spotlight. Ever since I was on the covers of *Rolling Stone* and *Newsweek*, the paparazzi were following me and some of the media attention was not flattering or accurate; I felt I needed to warn her that it wasn't always easy or fun.

But in the tumult, there were bright spots. In 2003, Tammy and I decided to push back against all the divisiveness about same-sex marriage and planned a huge wedding! It was a beautiful white wedding with about two hundred of our closest friends and family. Al Gore came, Tom Hanks and Rita Wilson, Jennifer Aniston, and Kate Capshaw and Steven Spielberg.

I wanted to live in the exuberance that was inside me after my awakening. I wanted to celebrate and play after such a long stretch of heaviness, heartache, and confusion. I've got to admit, many of the songs on *Lucky* were me pushing a *fake it 'til you make it* stance for sure.

Songs like "Kiss Me" capture my mood at the time:

Baby, whatcha doing tonight?
I'll go anywhere that you wanna go
I'll jump into my car
Go down to that bar
Pretend I'm someone that you don't know
I'll ask you if you would like to dance
Slip myself up close to your thighs
You can buy me a drink
We'll make everyone think
That love is so damn perfect tonight
Kiss me, kiss me
Kiss everything away
Oh, honey, now kiss me
Kiss me
Kiss me, come out and play
A woman can go crazy I know
Workin' all day in and day out
We'll let off some steam
Create a scene
Nothing like a good scream and shout

I wanted to make things simple and play some naughty rock and roll.

But life really wasn't that simple for me. I had found this portal into Spirit, where love was everything, but I still had a lot of conflict and loose ends in my life. The separation agreement with Julie dragged on. Professionally I felt like I had to fight for my own vision, and underneath it all I had the gnawing fear that I was going to be left behind.

Although I had this desire to practice loving myself and living a life that stayed close to Spirit, I still didn't know how. I was living a kind of half life—half of me completely changed, the other half wondering if I had what it took to rise to the opportunity gifted to me.

When it was time to go on the road with *Lucky*, I was determined to make the most of it, regardless of the industry. I'd put together an amazing rock-and-roll band with Kenny Aronoff on drums, Philip Sayce on guitar, and Mark Brown on bass—it was one of the most high-octane rock bands I'd ever played with.

We'd decided to make it a smaller club tour. I didn't want to go from one big arena to another; I wanted to play in smaller venues and really connect with the audience—I needed that fix of performing up close in a personal way and feeling my music with my audience. We'd play five or six nights in a small city and then move on to the next. We rocked it!

Though I was having a blast on tour, I was also getting more and more frustrated with the record company who wanted to promote the only song on the album that I didn't write.

My feelings of resentment forced me to confront what was important to me. It helped me to remember that as much as I was changing, I was still dealing with past hurts and having difficulty breathing through the pain. It might have taken someone else to write a song that would help me to see something I couldn't access in myself. Once I had that realization, I turned that resentment into gratitude. Maybe Spirit was working its way through me in ways that weren't immediately recognizable.

Toward the end of the fall of 2004, as I was wrapping up the *Lucky* tour, I was set to play one more show at a casino in Ottawa. I wanted the audience to rock with me—I wanted to get up on that stage and see the energy in the room go electric. I wanted to raise the roof.

Well, that didn't happen.

I looked out at the lovely audience, and everyone looked sedated. *Seriously*, I asked myself, *what am I doing here?*

My own energy just went down into my feet, and I felt as if a slow-moving iceberg was about to smother me, pushing me under. I am never not excited when I perform, but that night, I felt like I had reached some kind of low point.

After the show, I went back to my room and looked up at the ceiling from the lonely hotel room bed and asked the universe, "What do you want from me?"

The next morning in the hotel shower, I found a lump in my breast.

You might think I freaked out. That feeling a mass the size of a small tampon made me sweat with fear. You might think I started to cry.

Except none of that happened.

No—I felt that lump and I said to myself, *This isn't what I had in mind.*

The lump was big—about six centimeters—and up high on my left breast. How could I have not felt it before? Was I not paying attention? I had been out of touch with my body for those few years, and it was definitely not letting me ignore it any longer.

It wasn't like I didn't worry—I did. But I had this other level of awareness, like I was plugged into a different socket. Spirit, I was learning, often comes to light through darkness.

*   *   *

Thoughts of cancer are different from the reality of cancer. I knew I could get myself worked up about all the bad things that could happen. I could think about not being around to watch my kids grow up. I could think about no longer being able to play music. I could think about dying. But I had this strong sense deep inside that none of those fears would come to pass. At least not yet.

I went to see a radiologist who was also a friend. She brought me into the examining room, took out a very long needle, and inserted it into my left breast. It became stuck when she was trying to withdraw it. It hurt, but I tried to smile at her friendly face.

She looked at me and said, "We will have to wait for the biopsy results, but I've seen enough of these to tell you this: it's cancer."

I appreciated her honesty and her directness. I was a big girl; I could handle it.

Then very casually, she opened her white doctor jacket and said, "This is the worst that will happen." She was showing me her bare chest, revealing a double mastectomy.

I had surgery soon after, a lumpectomy. I went to a surgeon who was kind of grumpy, but recommended by our family naturopathic doctor. The surgeon explained that she first had to pull out the cancer from the sentinel node to see what stage I had. They told me I had stage-three cancer. I didn't really care about the number. I was paying attention to how they talked to me about the cancer.

A few days later, I had to have a second surgery to clear the margins, the area around where the mass had been removed. They had found cancer in the sentinel node, and the surgeon explained that she wanted to make sure the cancer wouldn't spread further into my lymph nodes.

We have approximately eight hundred lymph nodes throughout our bodies. When cancer cells migrate to our lymph nodes, we are much more vulnerable to the cancer spreading. As the grumpy surgeon explained all of this to me, she also mentioned that I might want to invest in a wig. The surgery wasn't going to cause my hair to fall out, but the chemotherapy that followed the surgery would surely do that for me.

I looked at her incredulously. "Do I look like someone who's going to wear a wig?"

She offered this unwelcome advice in response: "No one wants to look at a bald rock star."

Cancer hurts.

This wasn't my first encounter with the disease. My dear grandma Annie Lou had died of breast cancer when I was a child. My dad died of liver cancer when I was thirty years old. When he was diagnosed, I moved my parents out to Los Angeles so my father could get state-of-the-art medical treatment. I also wanted to be near him. The cancer had spread quickly, ravaging his body and draining his energy. They settled into a lovely condo near to where Julie and I were living at the time. In his final months, I spent as much time as I could with him. I'd tell him what I was up to, how my career was shaping up, and I also told him as often as I could how much I loved him. He got irritable sometimes, but I knew that was not the real him—it was the pain or the drugs talking. I'd just sit beside him and say my own kind of prayer, singing to him softly and playing the old Stella he'd brought home so long ago.

My dad had always been my biggest fan and most steadfast cheerleader. I knew that his belief in me made all the difference. From him, I learned to believe in the essential goodness of people. He was kind and loving, patient and engaged, a thoughtful, caring teacher who walked his talk. I internalized his love for me, and I know it gave me the courage to believe in my dreams and believe in my music, especially when there were darker forces at work in my life. I think he knew that music was a lifeline, a way to take myself seriously. I was beginning to sense that music might do for me what others in my life couldn't—help me understand myself.

Before my dad passed, I told him that I would take care of my mom and my sister. I was happy to watch out for my mom, but when it came to my sister, it was a promise I would later regret. Jenny only contacted me when she needed something, mostly money. Besides my anger with her, I hated the part of me that enabled her selfishness.

By that time, I had told my mother about Jenny's behavior toward me, but I don't think she ever really believed me—she didn't want the responsibility of having done nothing to prevent it. After my dad passed, my mother reminded me once again to put Jenny before me.

I was mourning the loss of my father and not thinking clearly. But the more I revisited my mother's command, the more it grated. How could she ask me to take care of my abuser? How could she ask me to mother Jenny, when she couldn't mother either one of us?

I felt a surge of anger and resentment course through me. I hated them both at that moment. My dad, my angel, had died. Wasn't I allowed some comfort? Was my mother not capable of any compassion toward me?

As I sat contemplating my own cancer diagnosis, these thoughts and memories returned with great precision. I didn't want to be that angry, resentful person anymore. I didn't want to die with regrets or untapped desires, and I didn't want to blame others for my feelings and shirk my responsibilities. I was beginning to understand that living in Spirit meant standing in my own truth, not in the shadows of others.

*   *   *

I had the surgery in October 2004, and then I had to wait two weeks to heal before I started chemotherapy treatment. I had spoken to a few oncologists about treatment options. It seemed like every one of them wanted to explain why cancer happens: Cells go bad. Cells go rogue. No one was trying to explain *why* cells go bad, though.

Tammy came with me to my first chemo appointment, the day after Halloween—All Souls Day for some. We'd had a raucous time taking the kids trick-or-treating the day before. Bailey and Beckett were dressed as the opposite gender—they were seven and six at the time. I was in full-blown clown gear. The next day would prove much more somber.

When we arrived at the hospital, Tammy was shaking and so upset that the nurse gave her a Valium—not the support I needed as I sat there for hours with an IV filling my body with liquid poison.

I realized that Tammy was probably not going to be able to handle my treatment, so I called Steven, one of my best friends and tour manager, who then stayed by my side for each and every treatment appointment and follow-up visit. Steven is like a brother to me; without even me having to ask, he put down the tour book and picked up the cancer book.

Once, early on in the chemo, I drove by myself down to LA for treatment and was feeling pretty positive. I relished being alone, and driving always put me in a good headspace. Meditating on Spirit, I tried to stay open and mentally nimble—all positive manifestations.

On the way home, not so much.

I wanted to stop and vote in the presidential election between George W. Bush and John Kerry. I hadn't changed my address yet and needed to vote in advance in Brentwood. Driving back, I was thinking to myself, *I don't feel well at all.* I got in bed as soon as I reached home and I didn't get out for a week.

Chemo feels like you're drinking liquid fire. It burns through your insides, which is exactly what it is intended to do. Today, not all chemo is that gnarly or dangerous. But back then in 2004, they were using treatments that hadn't changed in thirty years. It was barbaric. They made the poison from poison—literally a chemical that was left over from World War II that was similar to mustard gas. The military medics wanted to find another use for it and discovered that if it was injected into our veins, it would kill every living, dividing cell. It will keep your cells from dividing. So the thought was, well, if you have cancer cells dividing, it will kill those also. I know it made sense at the time when the main objective was to kill the cancer by any means necessary. But that didn't mean they had considered just how vicious chemo was.

The nurses inserted a port in my chest through which the chemo could go straight into the heart, so the heart could then pump it through the bloodstream throughout my body.

After being diagnosed, I worried about Bailey and Beckett. They were both super-sensitive little creatures and I didn't want them to see me so strung out and tired. I arranged the custody visits so they would see me the week after the chemo effects would lift, before my next treatment. Before they arrived, I would get out of bed, put on some clothes and a baseball hat, and we'd go outside to the big backyard behind the house. I tried to time their visits for when I had the most energy so they wouldn't notice that I was not their normally energetic mom. We'd hang outside and I'd watch them play.

But they knew something was up, and I wanted them to understand that I was not dying. I told them, "You know Mama is sick. It's like I have a cold inside my body. There was a lump that was taken out so that it won't make me sick anymore. Now I have to take this medicine that makes me look weird, but it's good. It will make sure the lump doesn't come back."

Beckett came to me one day and asked me, "Mama, are you going to still be sick when I'm sixteen? Because I really want to ride bikes with you again."

When I lost all my hair and was looking all gray, Beckett said, "Mama, you look like a vampire." And I laughed.

During the visits where I couldn't get it together to play with them, Bailey, sweet baby, would come in and sit at the end of the bed and hold my hand and not say a word.

Beckett seemed to have a harder time. I told him that I wouldn't look like this for long, but it was really hard on him. They were bouncing back and forth between my house and Julie's, which was hard enough.

The protocol for chemo was eight sessions, one every two weeks, which meant it was going to be four months of hell. I was on Adriamycin, nicknamed the Red Devil—an intravenous cancer medicine, which has since been discontinued—and yes, it's bright red and just as horrible as it sounds. After one treatment, it felt like my bones were going to break in two. I peed red. I lost my hair. I lost my sense of taste. My gut was a mess. The only thing that gave me some relief was cannabis. So in the week after a treatment, when I was feeling my worst and the kids were not around, I would smoke all day long, just to feel normal, to rest, and to trigger an appetite. People stop eating during chemo because your whole system is just whacked.

The cannabis took the edge off the pain in an almost immediate way. But there were times after a session of the next drug they gave me—Taxol—where even the cannabis wouldn't help with the pain. They prescribed opioids in pill form and these terrible-tasting suckers, but I honestly don't remember what they contained. I tried one once and spit it out immediately—that had been my one and only direct exposure to opioids.

One day when Steven was visiting, I turned to him and said, "I want you to call the doctors and I want you to ask them what's the chance of this cancer coming back if I don't continue with three more of these sessions."

I was supposed to undergo another month and a half of treatment.

Steven made the call and reported back to me, looking at me lying in my bed, the covers bunched up around my chest and neck.

"The doctor said that the chance of the breast cancer recurring was only 4 percent more than the average rate."

I looked at Steven, who had been my rock the whole time, and I said, "I quit. I'm willing to take the risk. And I'm not willing to go through this torture any longer."

And that's what I did: I quit. I knew full well that my decision was against the advice of the medical experts, but I'd had enough of the misery of treatment. And I'm happy to say that I've been cancer-free and healthy for over twenty years.

CHAPTER 8

A GUT FEELING

After that decision to stop chemo, I was energized and determined not to simply beat cancer, but to address it. I started reading again, this time about how and why cancer starts. I understood that the cancer cells are like rogue cells that take on a life of their own, attacking the body from within. I also understood that the way I was living–high stress, bad American diet, little balance–wasn't helping matters. I delved into mind-body medicine and researched ways to manage my anxiety and stress so they wouldn't trigger inflammation or disease. I was trying to understand the root cause of cancer cells and discovered that the gut plays a crucial role in helping the innate immune system keep cells in check–letting certain cells die so they don't become cancerous. I also learned that a gut in a chronically acidic state causes an inflammatory process called senescence, causing cells to stop dividing, and can be a precursor to the cells becoming cancerous.

The body's innate intelligence astounded me. The more I read about cancer and what happens at the cellular level, the more I understood how cancer and other inflammatory diseases can be prevented with a clean diet that keeps the gut more alkaline and less acidic—in other words, ph-balanced. At the time, there were not many books that described nutritional healing for cancer—I was finding content in handbooks at health-food stores that was all very cutting-edge and not at all mainstream, but I remember it making so much sense, especially since I had struggled with gut issues for such a long time. Instead of using poison to kill the cancer, maybe I should try to fix my gut.

I began a new regimen and promised myself that I would stay away from the crap food. I remember one of my first meals of cut-up pineapple chunks over wild rice. It felt like liquid gold, just so soothing and calming on my whole system. I started sipping on hot water and lemon. I ate a ton of avocados and salads. I avoided dairy, white bread, and other packaged foods that all created an acidic overgrowth. I still eat this way to this day.

Not all my doctors agreed with my new protocol, but I felt optimistic and physically healthier from the new diet.

My close friend Linda really showed up for me during the time I was dealing with cancer treatments. She'd come over when I felt well enough for company, and we watched football together—something we still love to do. Some days I could barely speak, but I'd raise my hand and she'd gently raise hers.

Linda and I had been friends for a number of years, ever since she'd reached out to me to see if I'd be interested in doing a show for television. Linda had an amazing reputation as a director and showrunner—she was the genius behind *Nurse Jackie*, starring Edie Falco.

The show Linda and I had in mind never came to be, but we'd been close ever since, talking and emailing each other. I couldn't foresee just how close we'd get, but during this low point, Linda was a rock for me, someone I could talk to and vent with. She and Steven were true friends. They showered me with unconditional, beautiful love. Theirs was the sort of love that I'd longed for in my romantic relationships—but I hadn't been able to find that yet.

*   *   *

As I was working to bounce back post-treatment, the women in my life were creating some unwelcome challenges. Tammy, not the most patient person in the world, began talking again about wanting to have a child. She loved kids, and she was great with Bailey and Beckett. The stress started to mount.

In my head I thought, *Now?* But she had waited while I went through my ordeal with cancer, and it certainly wasn't a good time then, with me being sick and out of it for so long. I understood her urgency and I wanted to be supportive. Though I wasn't really feeling up to it, I ultimately acquiesced to Tammy, as was my pattern. Tammy started IVF treatment with an anonymous sperm donor. Part of me thought, *Okay, one more kid.*

As anyone who's gone through IVF will tell you, it's a difficult process—a tiny bit of hell that requires pumping a woman full of hormones that can radically affect moods. As I struggled to stay in no-stress mode to take care of my own healing, Tammy dove into IVF treatment. I tried to stay calm and clear, so my recovery would continue to improve, but there were days when I felt the weight of the strain. I was responsible for two households, my health, and my career—nothing seemed easy, despite my trying to take it all in stride.

The pressures continued to mount.

The custody and money battles with Julie continued. In one meeting, while I was still in the throes of chemotherapy, her lawyer got very aggressive, saying I was not well enough to parent Bailey and Beckett, and suggested that Julie receive full custody. I looked at the lawyer and then at Julie in total disgust. Were they really going to use my cancer diagnosis against me and my children? Who would do such a thing? I find it hard to fathom how people who you once loved, and who you thought loved you in return, can come at you with the intent to harm. I look for the love and compassion hiding in those circumstances, but admit I struggle to find it.

We had been doing a pretty good job of keeping our personal business out of the media—to protect our children and our right to privacy. I was also protective of my career and the assumptions people made about me being ill. Back then, at the turn of the twenty-first century, no one talked about cancer because if you got cancer many assumed you were going to die.

When Julie and her lawyer threatened to take my kids away from me, I simply got up and walked out of the meeting.

A few days later, I also received a letter from the bank that had agreed to give me a mortgage on a new house in Hidden Hills, the same neighborhood. The bank was telling me that because I was ill with cancer, they needed to withdraw their loan. I immediately called the loan officer and told him point-blank that if they acted on this threat, I would go to every news outlet in the greater Los Angeles area and tell them just how heartless the bank was. After our call, they quickly saw the error of their ways.

Through it all, I continued to work on my music—which always centered me. During chemo, I created most of the songs for the soundtrack of the children's film *Brother Bear 2*. Soon after I decided to ditch the chemo, I got a call from my manager, who asked me timidly, "Do you want to perform at the Grammys and do a tribute to Janis Joplin with Joss Stone?"

Heck yeah!

Tammy thought I was crazy, given the fact that I was still weak from the chemo, and bald as a cue ball.

But I was completely determined.

On that night, a bit shaky in my boots, I wondered if my voice would hold up and if I could finish the entire song. I had decided to sing "Piece of My Heart"—a song I loved to sing but I knew it would take a lot out of me.

So there I was up onstage in front of all my peers and then some, and I belted it out, wanting to do Janis justice and prove that something like cancer was not going to keep me down. It was just the kind of feat I needed to push me out of the sick mindset and embrace my present and future. Spirit was tangibly present by my side during that performance. I felt an incredible sense of victory!

Oh, and by the end of 2006? I was the very proud mother of twins: Johnnie Rose, a five-pound little girl, and a little boy, Miller Steven, who came in at five pounds and one-ounce.

Life had taken another turn and I was feeling good!

In 2005, in the middle of my battle with breast cancer, I'd been working with a yoga teacher. One day, surprising myself, I found myself manifesting, telling her, "I'm going to win an Oscar."

She didn't blink, but nodded, understanding that I was manifesting a desire, a goal for myself.

"I just want to say it out loud, so that when it happens, I will know that I've shared it with someone."

She was my witness.

So two years later, a couple of months after I sang at the Grammys, I was nominated for an Oscar for "I Need to Wake Up," a song I wrote and performed for Al Gore's documentary film, *An Inconvenient Truth*. The film won for Best Documentary that year as well. I couldn't believe it all, but then, I could.

That night, dressed in my navy-blue suit sitting among all sorts of Hollywood stars, I watched as my friend Ellen DeGeneres, the host, introduced two more friends—Queen Latifah and John Travolta. As they announced the nominees, I said to myself, "They're going to say my name. Oh my God, it's happening," and I started to giggle.

John Travolta announced the winner, saying my name, and I stood up, leaned down, and kissed Tammy on the lips. As far as I know, it was the first lesbian kiss at the Oscars! Another victory.

I walked up to the podium, the Oscar in my hand, and I thanked Tammy, I thanked all the people who had supported me throughout my career, and then I thanked Al Gore, who had shown me, truly, that saving our planet was not a red or blue issue—he showed me that we are all green. Amen to that.

What a night. I won a freaking Oscar!

Later that night following the award show, Tammy and I went to the *Vanity Fair* Oscar party, where I smoked a joint with Bill Maher, Sean Penn, and Harry Dean Stanton. Just one of those Hollywood moments!

I was moving and shaking and starting to believe that the future was mine to create if I just believed, believed in the love and practiced that love.

I did not seek out these opportunities; they came to me. That's how Spirit works. My new path was becoming increasingly clear to me. I could see that the best thing any of us can do is find peace within ourselves, and stay aligned within ourselves. Sure we can encourage others to do the same, but as Gandhi said, be the change you want to see. That's what I was trying to capture when I wrote "I Need to Wake Up":

Have I been sleeping?
I've been so still
Afraid of crumbling
Have I been careless?
Dismissing all the distant rumblings
Take me where I am supposed to be
To comprehend the things that I can't see
'Cause I need to move
I need to wake up
I need to change
I need to shake up
I need to speak out
Something's got to break up
I've been asleep
And I need to wake up
Now
And as a child
I danced like it was 1999
My dreams were wild
The promise of this new world
Would be mine
Now I am throwing off the carelessness of youth
To listen to an inconvenient truth
That I need to move
I need to wake up
I need to change

I need to shake up
I need to speak out
Something's got to break up
I've been asleep
And I need to wake up
Now
I am not an island
I am not alone
I am my intentions
Trapped here in this flesh and bone
And I need to move
I need to wake up
I need to change
I need to shake up
I need to speak out
Something's got to break up
I've been asleep
And I need to wake up
Now
I want to change
I need to shake up
I need to speak out
Oh, something's got to break up
I've been asleep
And I need to wake up
Now

Cancer turned out to be another sign from the universe that change was upon me. I was not afraid. I did not want to wallow in self-pity. I wanted this new spiritual force that was growing in and around me to help me reframe this scary word and make it into a launching pad from which to learn. Cancer had required that I develop a new way for me to think about my body and live in it—yes, it was a forced lesson, but ultimately one that I came to value. I now understood that I had to treat my body with a sacred attention. And though I was a body, I was also spirit. I was filled with the sacredness of life and the wonder of creation. I was beginning to understand that any change has the potential for transformation and though I wish it on no one, the extremity of the cancer, of getting so sick and feeling so helpless at times, made me succumb to the truth that I could not problem-solve my way out of the disease—instead, I had to surrender to cancer and trust that I was going to be okay. I was not minimizing the danger, but instead learning to stop trying so hard to control the outcome—that part of me that wanted so badly to solve my own and everyone else's problems since I'd been a kid.

One day, a few years after my cancer ordeal, I turned to Steven and said, "I think I need to see a shaman."

Later that same day, Steven sent me an article via email about an ancient ceremony called ayahuasca. Literally a few minutes after I received that article, I got an email from a fellow musician friend who invited me to an ayahuasca journey led by a shaman.

That's how this channel works. When you're open, life happens for you, not to you.

Gathered together were about ten people, including me and my friend who was hosting the ceremony. Also present were the shaman, who was French but who had studied in South America, and his two assistants. At his instruction, we had arranged ourselves on the floor, each of us to a yoga mat.

He described what was going to happen: each of us would sip from a liquid that had been prepared by blending the vine of the *Banisteriopsis caapi* and a shrub called *Psychotria viridis* found in the Amazonian rainforest. Indigenous tribes have been using the mixtures for purposes of deep physical and emotional healing for centuries, if not longer, and more recently others have been replicating the ceremony to promote insight, release from traumatic experiences, and reversing illness and disease. I did not go into this first experience with a precise intention; I was a total newbie, but I was incredibly curious to see what I would see. I was looking for healing in a general way, but other than that I was not focused on solving any specific problem, per se.

The shaman told us the plant medicine's intensity would more than likely make us purge and generally feel sick—all with the purpose of clearing the way for the insight that might come from reliving difficult or painful experiences. This ceremony was meant to connect us to the plant itself, putting us into an altered state where we would then go into the journey. He explained that it would take about thirty minutes for the thick brown tea to take effect.

Whereas with cannabis I was aware of the feelings it produced, in this case I didn't know what to expect from the ayahuasca ceremony. At that point, I had not read about it and didn't know anyone personally who had experienced it yet.

After thirty minutes had passed, I began to feel transported into a sphere of darkness. I saw myself climbing within an elaborate jungle gym, with light finding its way through prisms. The energy of the space was occupied with emotion—a visceral elation and joy, which then made me giggle. I looked to my friend and got up to sit close to her.

The shaman gave us the signal that this journey was meant to be singular; it wasn't about a shared experience. We had to separate and go back to our mats.

Then the mental sensations became more intense.

The shaman began to chant Icaros—ancient medicine songs calling upon Aya, the spirit of the plant, the grandmother spirit, who guides the journey.

I was both afraid and unafraid and let myself become part of the visions that were taking place in my head. I saw exquisite geometrical shapes and experienced a profound feeling of love and oneness—the English language is limited in how I can describe this ocean of sensation and deep emotion—I saw myself on a swing in my backyard. I saw myself under the bed, as if trapped. I felt myself floating on a raft in the middle of an ocean.

After that night, I was left feeling a new kind of awareness of and connection to myself and my surroundings. Coming forth in my mind was an emerging embodiment of understanding, but this was wider, deeper, more intense, and lasting.

* * *

All of this shifting of my consciousness was coming together in *The Awakening*. The album is a lyrical chart of my life—a spiritual narrative—that traces my early life in Kansas discovering myself in music, battling my sense of injury from my mother and sister, then moving out to California. From there, I recounted my turbulent relationships, becoming politically aware, and the birth of my kids. Ultimately the songs, in their particular order, are a message of intention: *I don't want to hurt anyone, I don't want to stay stuck in the past.* I was waking up in the moment to the realization that all we can really do is love one another, as one of my songs says:

> *All we can really do*
> *Is love one another*
> *All we can really do*
> *Is love one another*
> *All we can really do*
> *Is love one another*
> *All we can really do*
> *Is love one another*
> *Yeah, all we can really do*
> *Is love, love, love one another*

Looking at my life from this new perspective made it clear that the yin and yang of it all are what promise its beauty and its forgiveness. Sure, some bad, painful things happened, but alongside the dark came the light. This helped me to look at cancer as an opportunity. It enabled me to look at my past relationships not as concrete blocks of pain, but rather as moments in my long stretch of life that once held weight but were no longer heavy. I was letting go of baggage. I was letting go of stuff that didn't serve me or the higher good.

I seemed to be attracting people who wanted to change the world. This is why Al Gore had reached out to me for his documentary film, *An Inconvenient Truth*. This is why I was being asked to stand up for justice, for the environment, for peace. I continued to be invited to contribute to a number of causes—gay rights, climate change, world peace. I performed at the Live Earth concert at Giants Stadium in July 2007 and later that year traveled to Oslo, Norway, to do a concert in honor of the Nobel Peace Prize. It was becoming more and more important for me to show up for other people and give my time and money to do my part in making the world a better place. I had come to the conclusion that in order to keep growing as a person, I wanted to surround myself with people who were looking to make changes we all wanted to see. I wanted my work to be healing and helping; I wanted my music to be an uplifting part of people's lives.

THE UNIVERSE LISTENED

We do our best
We stay in step
As time goes marching by
But there's something wrong
We don't start living
Until we almost die
Yeah, yeah, yeah
The universe listens
I was born silver thorn
On a Midwest rose
Found out fast love is last
And it comes and goes
Made a deal
Hearts to steal
They will know my name

I will pay the price

Any price

Just give me the fame

Yeah, yeah, yeah

The universe listened

Perfect song

My love is wrong

So I ate the dark

A hero's close

The story goes on

But I hate the part

I chose to fall

Destroy it all

But I will rise again

I believe in love

Please send me love

And I will try again

Yeah, yeah, yeah

And the universe listened

Yeah, yeah, yeah

And the universe listened

Remove the dark

Peel my heart

Make my body whole

I found my angels

Found my spirit

Guess I found my soul

Teach me how

Show me now

This light has taken me
I'm not ashamed
Help me explain
This awakening
Yeah, yeah, yeah
And the universe listened
Yeah, yeah, yeah
And the universe listened

So I was choosing love, or I should say, I was practicing to choose love, every day. All the songs on *The Awakening* album come from this new place. "Message to Myself" is about finding what you seek, asking for love, and how fear can make us weak. It zeroes in on what I was discovering: that truth is what we really seek—that's the human urge, the drive to know. That's what so many of the mystics and spiritual teachers and healers were talking about.

In my song "California," I was capturing my belief that love was possible:

I will find my love
I will know my peace
I will seek my truth
I am almost free

By the end of that album, I am no longer wrestling with the longing for love, I am declaring to myself and the world this new worldview that was grounded in love.

It was all beginning to make sense to me.

CHAPTER 9

ROCKS IN THE ROAD

No parent likes to think that their child will be unhappy or sad in their life. We start families and raise children with hope and love and a desire to protect them, knowing, too, that challenges and disappointments and disruptions are inevitable. My children certainly witnessed some of my struggles—with breakups, health issues, a career that wasn't always on track with my ambition. Front of mind during all of these trials was remaining present for each of my four children while also, like all working mothers, trying to balance career, life's challenges, and motherhood. I was going through an intense emotional and spiritual transformation that kept me heady and off-balance, but my kids were my priority, and knowing that helped to keep me grounded.

When Bailey and Beckett came to me for a week at a time, the house would get a little crazy. The twins were toddlers and they adored their older siblings, and Bailey and Beckett were just as nuts about the twins. Bailey and Beckett were nine and eight at this point. After the twins were born, Tammy had become a no-nonsense house captain, trying to assert order in a busy and chaotic household. The older kids did not like this new version of Tammy. And no matter how hard we tried, there were always toys, diapers, sippy cups—you name it—scattered around the house. Oh, and we had a dog. Indoor/outdoor living meant lots of dust bunnies and mud tracks and other things from outside making their way inside.

I was busy working on a Christmas album and new songs for the *Fearless Love* album. These and some other projects took me on the road. My absence did not help the tensions that were building between Tammy and me. We were fighting a lot, and Bailey and Beckett were absorbing the conflicts—both at home with Tammy and me, and at Julie's.

Part of me wanted to hide from the schisms that were becoming hard to ignore. It had been so hard with Julie, and now, with two more children, I dreaded the drama of another breakup—both personally and publicly. I so wanted to have a family that was more in sync than not. A family that worked through the rough spots. I also wanted to model a happy gay family. Maybe that was my ego talking, maybe that was a responsibility I put on myself, but the situation felt loaded, and the pressure was building around our sweet family.

I had also begun to worry about Beckett. Earlier, on his second birthday, we had given him a party. It was mostly grown-ups, with some other kids there as well. We had given him a Thomas the Tank Engine table. We'd put it in the middle of the room along with other small gifts. We were a small group, and everyone was singing and laughing and having a great time. I was standing off to the side, looking at Beckett as he stared at his present, a toddler-sized table with toy trains, with a face that said, *God, I hate this*. It wasn't fear, exactly; it was more just plain discomfort. I imagine he didn't love the crowd of people, and I realized that I had to pay more attention to the kind of socializing he was comfortable with.

As he got older, he was most happy when it was just the two of us—walking the trails around our house, riding bikes together. I'd take him skiing at Big Bear or fishing during vacations. There was nothing more satisfying to me than when Beckett would break into a smile, telling me he was happy.

But that wasn't often. It was far more common to catch him looking uncomfortable, a strained expression on his face.

One day Beckett and his elementary school class had a school outing to the beach. I had volunteered to chaperone and sat on the beach at the shoreline alongside a few other parents, keeping an eye on the kids. The ocean was rough, with a strong undertow. After one rather big tumble, Beckett emerged from the water with a smile and a wave. He ran toward me and stumbled into my arms as I wrapped a towel around him and held him to me.

In the car ride on our way home, he said to me from the back seat, "You know, Mom, when I got pulled down under the waves, I heard a voice say to me, *Just relax, you got this.*" And he smiled his beautiful smile.

Later that night, as I was tucking him into bed, I told him, "Beckett, that's your inner voice. You should always stay connected to it—that will lead you through life."

By the time Beckett reached middle school, his difficulty falling asleep had worsened. He'd be up late—two or three a.m.—wandering around the house. Julie took him to see doctors and therapists, who put him on meds for ADHD, but the medication did not help my little boy. Instead, it seemed to make him more uneasy and more uncomfortable in his own skin and cemented his belief that something was wrong with him—the seeds of shame I knew so well.

I often thought that if only I could just help him stay in that place he found in the ocean that day and listen to his own inner voice.

Sometimes he'd get obsessed with a new interest. For a while it was cars, then it was watches, and later on it was with muskets and World War II guns and rifles. But he was never satisfied with anything for very long. He was a smart kid—you could see that in how he dived into whatever he was interested in. School, though, made no sense to him. He couldn't start an assignment or a project because he convinced himself it wouldn't be perfect. We sent him to a Waldorf school, which had an open curriculum that offers kids agency in choosing the subjects and classes they preferred, so they would be more engaged in the work. But that didn't matter. Regardless of the class, the content, or the situation, Beckett could not connect as a student. He just couldn't do anything the teachers asked of him.

His teachers didn't quite know what to make of him or how to help him. He was a child who needed the right attention, but the system was not equipped to figure out how to address his needs. No matter how patient or psychologically minded his teachers were, they diagnosed him as being oppositional defiant, lacking in focus, and behaviorally challenged. This was not an incorrect assessment of his behavior, but what was underlying the behavior? We were all at a loss to find a solution. I think today we are further along than we were fifteen years ago in our collective understanding about how we can help these kids who don't fit the mold of the average student, the average child—alas, we know now that an average anything is a myth. The language and expertise of understanding

Beckett's unique profile as a student and his trouble regulating neurobiologically wasn't there yet.

In an effort to smooth over the general negativity of Beckett's school experience, I'd take him on tour with me. He loved being on the road, moving from place to place, and having me to himself. He loved living on my tour bus, and I felt him calm with the simplicity of the routine of our days and nights. He loved discovering new towns and hanging out at the lighting board during shows. His bunk was right above mine, and I listened as he slept with ease.

But back at home, in his so-called normal routine, Beckett struggled. I can see him sitting at the big round table in our open kitchen, his books and notebooks strewn around him. I'd rummage around the kitchen, preparing a snack for him, trying not to hover. But he'd be unable to focus, unable to do any homework. I found myself repeating, "Beckett just pick up the pencil," like it was a mantra.

When Julie brought him to a psychiatrist in LA, who diagnosed Beckett with ADHD and prescribed Ritalin, we trusted he, as part of the medical establishment, knew best. But a little voice inside me questioned why a stimulant would be good for a kid who already had trouble sleeping and whose anxiety was palpable.

It was around this time, when Bailey was about to turn thirteen and Beckett was twelve, Beckett got caught smoking weed at school. I tried to help him understand that his brain was too vulnerable for him to smoke cannabis and that even though it wasn't scientifically a gateway drug, it was not good for him. Of course, he knew I enjoyed cannabis, which didn't help matters, and I'm sure caused him confusion. He was not old enough or mature enough to see the difference. Perhaps I had been too lax in my own use. Bailey was exposed as well, but didn't feel the need to engage. One child's response has nothing to do with another's, though—I learned this the hard way—and I began to keep my cannabis use private, away from him.

He resented our disciplining him and started to push against everything, especially Tammy, who had become very strict. I didn't know where to turn.

Things came to a head in 2009, when Bailey was in eighth grade and Beckett was struggling to stay in seventh grade. The tension had been increasing between Julie and Bailey, who had asked to live with me full-time. Beckett was more flexible, but he could be persuaded by his older sister. I didn't know what to do.

Bailey and Beckett came to me with a mediator, who basically said, "Look, the kids want to be with you full-time, but they don't want to be there with Tammy."

My options were crushing. I either had to end my relationship with Tammy, which was hard, especially because the twins were two years old, or carry on, knowing that I was putting my other children through hell.

Then one night, we were all in the kitchen when Tammy began shouting and the kids, now frightened, visibly recoiled from her. I was trying to reason with Tammy, the twins were becoming more and more agitated, and then Tammy lost her shit with Bailey. I turned to the older kids and said, "We're leaving the house. Let's go."

Once we were in the car, I said to Bailey and Beckett, "Okay, we're going to do this. It's just going to be the three of us for a while." I didn't really know what that meant or how to do it, but I needed to be clear for them. My divine contract.

That blowup happened in September of 2009. By October,

Tammy had moved out. The twins were about to turn three years old.

At first, I was relieved, until she threatened to take the twins away from me. She wouldn't even let me see them for a few months. I was engaged in yet another custody and settlement battle. Tammy wanted money (a lot of money) and full custody of the twins. I laid out a demand that was also a plea. "Please don't make me do this. We each get joint custody of the twins. Let's be reasonable adults here and do what's best for our children."

We reached an initial arrangement, and Tammy agreed to fifty-fifty custody. Then the kids started coming over every other week and we settled into a schedule.

I was always trying to smooth things over between my older kids and Tammy, which led to fights because she felt I was undermining her, which I guess I was. I had tried so hard to be openhearted and compassionate when Tammy and I were breaking up, trying to follow the energy of Spirit and voice of love. There is no greater test than when you are under threat, hurt, and angry. That's when you find out if you can live up to what's been offered to you. I wanted to extend that love toward her even in the midst of the fighting and disagreements. I didn't always succeed, but I do think I found it in myself at times, and it certainly mitigated the tension and helped us to come to an agreement.

On the heels of Tammy leaving, I was now up to my eyeballs with pressure to make things happen. I was supporting two households, outside of my own, including child support. When the kids were with me, I was on my own.

Beckett was a continued source of worry. Bailey had decided to go to boarding school, so she was no longer there to absorb the tension and my anxiety. I was trying to figure out how to help him:

He'd been caught again with drugs at school—this time Xanax and cocaine. He was trying to medicate his way out of pain. By the end of eighth grade, he'd been kicked out of school. We sent him to a boarding school briefly, but he was asked to leave there, too. Then, since he loved being outside so much, we decided to send him to a wilderness program. He went to three different wilderness programs over the next couple of years, and though he found relief and some happiness in these back-to-nature places, he'd come home from each program, and reentry was not easy.

One day when I was venting to Linda, I asked her if she could come help out. She'd been living in New York and was wrapping up work there before she went on hiatus from showrunning the hit series *Nurse Jackie*. She had also told me she had been thinking about selling her house in Los Angeles.

Linda had for so long been a constant, calming, and steadying presence in my life. She had a great sense of humor and got along really well with Julie and with Tammy. She could neutralize tensions among us and lighten up any room. She'd always come over and spend Sundays with us. Sometimes she'd bring a girlfriend. And she loved football as much as I did. Linda was a balm in my life in every way.

Linda and I had a years-long friendship that showed us that we shared a similar outlook on life. She was on her own awakened path and wanted to live a more spiritually centered life. Like me, she was a seeker, unafraid to ask tough questions and follow her curiosity. We were both also trying to live healthier lifestyles. We were on the same track.

Linda was also one of my favorite people to play my music for. She would always tell me her true opinion of it, and I respected her musical instincts. She had a built-in sense of the integrity of a piece of music or a song. I remember clearly one time when I wanted her to listen to a song I'd written, "Company," that eventually went on my *Fearless Love* album.

I'd been making the album in 2009, before the split with Tammy, and had rented a house in Malibu to get some space to create. On one particular night, I'd invited Linda to spend the night. There was this huge, oversized bedroom that was almost eight hundred square feet. I was on one end of the bedroom, on one bed, and she was on another bed.

She listened as I sang and played,

> *And all I want is company*
> *Someone to understand this misery*
> *Send a reflection of myself to me*
> *'Cause everybody needs some company*

I was singing this, and I finished the song, and I looked up and she was just in tears. I said, "Oh my God. Are you okay?"

And she said, "You just don't know what you've done," and she left the room.

In that moment I felt the depth of our connection.

And then she just, you know, let it go.

By then, she knew the kids really well—she had been one of the first to hold the twins after they were born. Linda had always been part of the texture of our lives, an important, stable presence. She was also one of the few people I could confide in, especially when my life would get messy. She never judged me or my partners. Even when I would go off on one of my tangents—she'd just listen and laugh. No judgment ever.

When my relationship with Tammy blew up, I felt embarrassed

and ashamed, partly because of the public scrutiny I feared, but also because I felt a certain sense of personal failure. I imagined the remarks in the press: *Here she goes again, some lesbian role model she is, unable to have a relationship that lasts!* In my worry and ruminations, Linda just let me have my feelings.

When Tammy left and the wheels were coming off at the house, I just didn't know how I was going to hold it all together. I was getting ready to tour for *Fearless Love*, and was really trying, but failing miserably, not to be stressed.

That's when I blurted out to Linda after she told me she was selling her house in LA: "Well, you can just come stay here? You can figure out what you want to do with your LA house and take time to decide what you want to do next."

Linda, being Linda, didn't hesitate. She said yes.

In early 2010, Linda moved into the office and slept on the pull-out couch.

She came to stay with me in January and February. And stayed through March and April, then May. Over those weeks, which turned into months, we fell into an easy routine. We'd get the older kids up, dressed, and fed, and then we'd drive them to school, a forty-five-minute round trip during which we talked and talked. Maybe it was because she's a Midwesterner like me. Or maybe it was our mutual love of football. Or maybe it was the fact that we were literally born on the same day, same year. Linda was born five hours earlier, which made her older—the first older woman I would ever date. Ha.

Each night, Linda helped me get the kids to bed. Then we'd sit up and continue to talk. She'd end up sitting in the bathroom with me while I took a bath. Our intimacy was growing—except for sex.

At the time, I didn't have much going on romantically, though there may have been a flirtation with a yoga teacher. But it had not occurred to me that Linda and I were heading in that direction.

Then slowly I began to realize that the trust and comfort that was building with Linda was what I had always yearned for in a partner. But I was so gun-shy, so afraid to jump into another relationship. All I could acknowledge to myself at the time was that with Linda, life felt easy. And I could use a little easy.

I invited her to come on vacation with us. I had bought a house in the Santa Fe area when I was with Julie, and before we figured out what to do with it, we'd go there for family holidays or vacations. Linda came with us on a couple of those trips, too.

In May, we planned a big party—we were both turning forty-nine, and we wanted to celebrate.

Soon after, we decided to host an ayahuasca journey. I had told Linda all about the first time I had journeyed and was eager to share this experience with her.

We had invited several close friends, people who were curious about plant medicine and the healing the ayahuasca ceremony was known to produce. The shaman had us all put down our mats and create our spaces.

The two of us went up to be close to the shaman. As we were situating ourselves, without thinking, we sat down next to each other.

And the shaman came up and said, "Partners should not sit next to each other."

Linda and I looked at each other and smiled, and said at the same time, "Oh no, we're not partners."

"Yes, you are," the shaman insisted. "I can see the energy between you. Maybe you don't know your partner—yet."

It was after that ayahuasca ceremony when I started to realize that I did have those kinds of feelings for Linda, despite my trying to ignore or squash them. I lost interest in the yoga teacher and thought to myself, *Could Linda be the one?* Then I fell into a kind of stalemate with myself. I didn't want to make yet another mistake, get caught up in a relationship that would ultimately fail and ruin a beautiful friendship at the same time.

About a month later, we were in the kitchen getting the kids packed up and ready to take them to school. "Hey, hon, where are the sippy cups?"

Linda looked up at me and said with a smile, "Well, dear, they're right here."

Oh boy, I thought to myself. *Something is definitely changing.*

A week or so later, we were hanging out back on the patio, seated next to each other on the sofa. It was summer—sweet air coming off the garden. The sun was setting, and we leaned into each other and kissed.

The kiss was just as sweet as the air around us. A perfect moment. But it terrified me. I literally got up and ran into the house like a scared teenage girl!

The next morning I came into Linda's room. I had washed strawberries and put them in a blue ceramic bowl. "Okay," I said, "let's try this. Let's be grown-ups."

And once again, Linda said yes.

We got married at the San Ysidro Ranch up in Montecito. It was a small but wonderfully romantic ceremony. All the kids were there, and it just felt so right, so real. And it was also totally legal!

CHAPTER 10

AGREEMENTS WE MAKE

As I was deepening my spiritual journey, my son's troubles were escalating. Beckett was about to turn sixteen. After Beckett was kicked out of school the previous spring, I had found a one-on-one tutoring program for him to finish out high school. I believed that without a high school diploma, he would be even more ill-equipped to find his way in the world.

But that fall of 2014, he just couldn't keep up. He was hanging out with other kids who were failing to thrive. His behavior was erratic—one minute he'd be the soft-hearted boy I knew, and the next an angry almost-man telling me to fuck off. I would remind myself to stay in my own truth and keep my boundaries clear. Yes, I could love him fiercely, but I tried not to get in the tangle with him and his tortured psyche. I seemed the only one who he trusted to show his pain. He lashed out at me—not Linda or his sister or the twins. I guess he targeted me because he thought I could take it. Or maybe he also felt angry and frustrated by my inability to help him find relief. I understood it on one hand, but that doesn't mean it didn't hurt. I was in pain with him and felt helpless.

Beckett still wandered the house at night, unable to sleep. He would finally fall asleep in the wee hours and then could never wake up in the morning to go to the tutoring program near where we lived. When he asked if he could go to a snowboarding camp in Mt. Hood, Oregon, I didn't hesitate. He'd gotten really into boarding over the past several years. I'd take him locally to Big Bear and then out to Northern Cal and Colorado with the whole family. He loved the freedom of snowboarding, loved its culture. He used to school me on the terminology: that he loved to take air—meaning doing big jumps. He aspired to be an airdog. He was proud that he could drop in—meaning he could drop into a half-pipe with ease. He was learning how to do a backside 180—an aerial trick where you make a 180-degree turn off the jump, leading with the heel side of your board.

Hearing him talk enthusiastically about anything made me hopeful, so I supported his going to the camp whole-heartedly. I also thought that spending a lot of time in nature would do him good.

And hallelujah!

He called from the camp and said he had met a group of guys who were on the Aspen snowboarding team. They were super cool and they thought he was an amazing boarder. I had not seen him so excited and confident in a long time, and I was thrilled for him. He called me every night to tell me about his day and I began to feel more hopeful.

After Christmas that year, he asked if he could move up to Aspen for the season. His plan was to practice with the guys and try and make it into the X Games, a big snowboarding event that drew internationally ranked snowboarders and a huge audience. Seeing him with such focus, I didn't care so much if he didn't stick with school. Him finding his passion was something I could get behind. It wasn't entirely unlike what I'd done in my life. His happiness did not depend on his level of education.

Beckett was all adrenaline, energy, and vibrancy. My heart skipped a beat when I thought that maybe he'd finally found his life's purpose, or at least some direction. In my mind's eye, I would see him soar into the air, his face alight with joy and freedom. He was fearless; that's what his friends said. I wondered to myself, *Maybe he's just not tethered to this earth.*

But in the late fall of 2015, right after he turned seventeen and it was already high season in Aspen, Beckett called us. He'd been in a snowboarding accident and broken his ankle. It was bad. He'd been training with some of the elite-level athletes and practicing tricks. Doing a jump, he lost his bearings and fell forty feet and landed on his head. Thank God he'd been wearing a helmet. But his ankle broke. The medics at the mountain treated him on-site and then brought him to the hospital.

The ER docs said he had a pretty bad concussion and that his ankle was broken in two places. Unfortunately, there's not much you can do to repair a broken ankle. But there is something you can do for the pain. The doctor who eventually released Beckett sent him home in a boot and with a prescription for Vicodin.

The doctors did not want him traveling, so he stayed in Aspen. He had an on-again-off-again girlfriend who seemed to be tending to him. But honestly, we didn't know what we didn't know. For instance, we didn't yet know that the on-call surgeon had set his ankle incorrectly, a mistake that prevented Beckett from ever being able to snowboard again at the level he had achieved.

When I visited him, he seemed okay. I encouraged him to come home. I didn't like the looks of the medicine bottles, and I could tell he was getting depressed. The one thing that had made him get up in the morning with any sense of joy was snowboarding, and that had come to a screeching halt. But he wouldn't budge. He wanted to be in his own place. He did finally come home that spring, and it was clear that he was hooked on painkillers. His face was ashen. He'd lost weight. There was a faraway gaze in his eyes, like a veil covering the young man inside.

I asked him about the pain, and he'd nod and say that it was a constant, but I could see he was trying to be okay. At that point, he thought he'd get better and be able to go back to Aspen next season, pick up where he left off. I hoped that being motivated to board again would keep him off the drugs.

I'd watched him hobble and wince with pain, and it made me think back to my chemo treatments. I remembered that creeping pain that just gets into your bones. It's the kind of pain that radiates and never seems to go away.

We didn't realize that he'd become dependent on OxyContin by then. He had always had social anxiety and depression, which made him angry. Anger was how he dealt with any kind of uncomfortable feeling. The way to dampen the anger was by numbing himself with drugs. What I didn't understand was that he was in a cycle of pain, both physical and emotional. He started buying opioids on the street when his prescriptions ran out.

*   *   *

After the shooting of forty-nine people at the gay club Pulse in Orlando, Florida, I sat down the very next day and wrote a song in honor of the victims of the terrible hate crime. Three days later, I released the song "Pulse" as a single. I wrote the song to help people heal from the tragedy and to bring awareness to the fact that LGBQT+ people were a target of hatred and violence. I started thinking not only about what happens when someone dies—that their pulse stops—but what the heart does when it pulses—brings life, attests to life.

When I wrote the song, I was thinking not only about the victims who were violated, I was also thinking about my son, who also felt himself to be a victim.

Everybody's got a pain inside
Imaginary wounds they fight to hide
How can I hate them
When everybody's got a pulse
I dream in a world that wants my soul
That tells me if I hate I can control
But I don't believe it
I cannot conceive it
Because everybody's got a pulse
I am human, I am love
And my heart beats with my blood
Love will always win
Underneath the skin
Everybody's got a pulse
Once again I hang my head to cry
I can't find the reason why they died
We will find the answer
Blowing in the wind

By summer of 2016, Beckett and his girlfriend decided to move north to Santa Cruz, where he thought he could get some work on a farm. I wanted to believe that Beckett was more or less back on his feet. He seemed motivated to get a job and make some money. He was going to be eighteen in November, and we thought that his desire for independence was a good sign that he was ready to take care of himself.

As with snowboarding, we thought it would be a good fit for him. He'd be working outdoors, earning his keep and some self-reliance. We found out soon enough that the drug scene in Santa Cruz was too close and too much of a lure for Beckett. Like the tragic progression of so many opioid addicts, he had moved from Vicodin to street Oxy and then to heroin. When we got wind of his ramped-up drug use, we told him to come home.

* * *

Meanwhile, I turned to my music for some relief. A few years earlier, Linda had encouraged me to play more lead guitar. With her support, I gave myself inner permission to work on becoming an even better musician and began playing with Pete Thorn, a Canadian guitarist known worldwide for his art. He was one of the most un-egotistical lead guitar players that I knew. He had observed that I wanted to play more guitar and offered his help. He suggested that I get an early 1980s Les Paul Custom, which I did, and SUHR amp, along with various pedals. I practiced scales again, just like a beginner. I played the blues. I wanted to improve, which made me work even harder. And I had a blast, but soon Pete had taught himself out of a job.

I had poured my guitar playing into the album *4th Street Feeling*, which was all about me looking back on my life with new eyes. I wanted the songs to capture a time in my life, when all my stuff could fit in the back of my Chevrolet. I was thinking about that first solo trip from Kansas to LA, ready to take on the world and find fame and fortune. I think in some ways that album captures me in a state of wishful thinking, for I definitely knew by then that life was never that simple. I consciously leaned into Spirit—and into love. With Linda by my side, that love came easy. I was indeed ready to love again. My song "Rock and Roll Me" says it for real:

I think I'm ready to try my hand at love again
Because in my darkest hour
In my darkest hour, baby
I could always call you friend
And it feels like you believe me
When you hug me and you squeeze me
And when I blush you tease me
When you tell me you're gonna please me
Come on, baby, rock and roll me
Take me in your arms and hold me, hold me, baby
I want to be your one and only
Baby, rock and roll me
All night long
Forgive me, baby, if I'm a little nervous now
I never had a first time with such a familiar touch
It's been a long, long, long, long, long time
And I've needed, I've needed this, so much

In 2014, I had released *This Is M.E.*, my first album through my own record company, M.E. Records. I had finally ended my long relationship with Bill Leopold. I wanted to reinvent all parts of my career, choose who I worked with at all levels. Dealing with so many managers, agencies, and lawyers was eating up my energy. I wanted to clean house, streamline, and give myself a fresh start. I felt unafraid to follow my instincts, a result of having Linda by my side, and Spirit running through me. I wanted to connect with the world in a new way. My song "A Little Bit of Me" gets to that feeling:

> *If you believed, if you tried*
> *It could be enough to know you were alive*
> *If you knew the truth it couldn't be denied*
> *It would change the world enough that you might find*
> *That the world goes round and around and around*
> *And everybody walks on common ground*
> *We gotta pull together if we're gonna pull through*
> *There's a little bit of me in a little bit of you*
> *The world goes round and around and around*
> *Everybody feels a little upside down*
> *No need to be afraid of anybody you see*
> *There's a little bit of you in a little bit of me*

SILENT GOOD-BYE

After my dad died, my mother decided to leave LA and moved to Bentonville, Arkansas, for about thirteen years. After I went through cancer, she wanted to be closer to me, so I bought her a nice home in a lovely retirement community in Palm Springs. She lived there until around 2008, when she reached out to me and said, "You know, Missy, I'm not myself anymore. I think my memory is getting a little soft."

I then found her a clean, well-staffed memory care home near me in California and moved her there, where I could visit her regularly. I was the only one left who could care for her. As her dementia progressed, my mom seemed more comfortable and less anxious, her worries taken away from her along with her memory. Sometimes I'd pick her up and bring her over to my house, and I'd tell her about how well Bailey was doing in school. What outdoor adventure was keeping Beckett out of trouble. She didn't ever ask about my music—that must have slipped her mind. But I was grateful that the antagonism between us had all but disappeared in her final years. She could no longer fight that fight, and I did not want to spend my energy on old stuff.

In 2016, my mom finally let go. I'm not sure she believed in God or an afterlife, but she did seem at peace. A few days before she passed, I visited her in the memory care home. I was about to go out on the road to do some shows, so I wanted to say good-bye. Linda was with me. By that time, my mom was clearly failing. She looked tired and barely had any energy. But she recognized me when I came into her room. I sat close to her by her bed, and I gently took her hand and said, "Hi, Mom—how are you doing today?"

"Missy," she uttered in a low, weak voice.

And then she took my hand to her mouth and kissed it.

She had never done that before. I was shocked by its sweetness. She loved me after all. Linda was by my side to witness the moment, so powerful and hard to capture in words.

A few days later I got the call that my mom had died.

I had bought two plots for my parents in Forest Lawn cemetery in Los Angeles. We had my mom cremated and buried next to my dad. There was no formal service. Just me and Linda to send her off. I didn't ask the kids to come—they really only knew her from afar, and it didn't seem honest. I didn't want them to pretend a loss they didn't really feel.

I called my niece to let her and my sister know my mother had died.

I thought about my old promise to my dad to watch out for Jenny, but I knew now that the best thing I could do for my sister was to let her feel the consequences of her choices. I owned her house, which gave her a roof over her head, but I decided not to do more.

After my mom passed away, Jenny contacted me via text: *Hey, Sis, can I borrow…*

I didn't respond immediately. Then I wrote her an email: *Do not contact me again. I will not give you any money.*

And that was it. My decision to stop sending any money to Jenny was huge for me. Although setting that boundary meant I felt more whole and honest with myself, it did not mean that I had forgiven her violation of me or the years of terrorizing me. I wanted to extend compassion—she had lost her son Joshua to opioids, an anguish no mother should have to withstand and one I feared, more than I could admit to, for myself and my own son. Still, I knew with certainty now that it was best for me to insist on this distance between us.

Now, I realize that my mom's death and the boundary that I had put between me and my sister meant that I had finally stopped clinging to the belief that I was a victim of my past circumstances. I could now accept that I was born into and raised in a complicated home. The trauma I endured from my sister and my mother's indifference were reflections and actions borne of their own limitations and pain. None of it was a reflection of me.

I often bring to mind a time driving with my mom and telling her that I wanted to be a musician. I asked her, "Do you think I can make it?"

"Well, it's a one-in-a-million chance, but who's to say you're not the one?"

Yes, she had her limitations, but I could also now admit, so did I. I reflect on Ruiz's fourth agreement: we must do the best we can do.

I began to see that my sister's violation of me set me up to normalize abusive behavior, to expect it or, at least, not reject it outright. It had been part of an embedded wiring, a legacy that was no longer necessary, and I had to untrain in myself. My dad did his best to offer me hope by being by my side as I toured around Kansas as a young girl, singing my heart out. I believe his way of trying to protect me was to take me away from the unhappiness of our home. Maybe my love for being on the road—the promise of escape—comes from these early trips away from my home with my dad. I also think that he protected me from more serious damage.

In the second half of my life, I began to integrate these pieces of my story.

Once again, I was gifted the opportunity to reconcile the good and the bad: my past and my present, the yin and yang. I had finally let go of the pain I had endured as a child.

*   *   *

Meanwhile, mothering continued to be hard work. It helped to have had this reconciliation and admission to the complications of motherhood as a way of forgiving my own mother. That, in turn, helped me from falling back on my compartmentalizing ways. I worked hard to stay present to the concerns about my kids when I was writing, making music, or on the road. Especially with Beckett. But music was also my refuge. I am made of music. Music made me. And through the process of creating I wrestled with myself, my worries and guilt about Beckett, with old, lingering shame that wanted to hold me back.

I confronted the fear that I was a fraud, a bad parent who couldn't help her troubled son. It was exacerbated by my fear of being exposed for my failure, how living in the spotlight meant I had to have this picture-perfect life. Of course that is absurd, but it still grated on my psyche. I thought I had moved on from the mode of self-referential thinking after enduring two public breakups. In the end, the anguish is personal; no one really cares about your life in any meaningful way. Everyone has their own demons to battle. Still, I was haunted by shame of exposure, surely a stubborn hangover from my childhood, and the specter that I was simply not a good enough mother. What that really meant is that I was terrified that I couldn't save Beckett. That fear was too much to face.

What if trying to do my best wasn't good enough? What then?

After the summer in Santa Cruz, Beckett came home and asked to go to rehab. It was just before he turned eighteen. He went in, he came out. This became a pattern: he wanted to get clean, committed to rehab or a treatment program, but never stuck it out long enough to do the real work of understanding his addiction and staying sober.

That next year, Beckett bounced around. Sometimes he stayed with his girlfriend, sometimes with one of his buddies. He got a job at a hotel in Aspen, determined to start the next snowboarding season with a bang. He hadn't really accepted that he would never board at a high level again. Sometimes I encouraged him to come home to visit, but we both knew that was shaky. His time at home had become stressful for all of us. We were either walking on eggshells trying to keep him calm, or he was blasting us with accusations and f-yous. I wanted to keep the door open to him. I wanted to say to him, *Of course, you're always welcome, this is your home.* But I could no longer depend on him being civil, and it wasn't fair to the household to have to tolerate his erratic behavior.

His job at the Aspen hotel didn't last. The pain of his injury lingered, and he couldn't really stand on his feet that long, so he left Aspen with some buddies and went up to Montana. He then spent time in Alaska and Wyoming. He sought out the places where he had gone to wilderness camp when he was younger. In Montana, he got a job landscaping for a while. But then he fell into using again, and eventually came back to California and we got him into another rehab program.

We didn't see him much in 2017, but now and again he'd turn up, saying he really wanted to get clean. He was an adult, and there was only so much we could do, legally or otherwise. By then, we'd asked him to stay at a hotel or with friends instead of with us. We felt it wasn't fair to the younger kids to see their older brother so messed up on drugs or to tolerate his belligerent behavior toward Linda and me.

It's torturous to sit powerlessly as a loved one struggles with addiction. They are not their true selves. They are not in charge of their decisions: the drugs are. Painkillers like Oxy trick the brain into thinking you need more, more, more, so that's all you can think of. The next fix. The next high. But the highs lose all their luster and there is no longer any pleasure to be had; it's been replaced by an impossible hole to fill. It's an endless cycle of pursuit, momentary relief, and disappointment. The addicted person no longer knows what's good for them. They become isolated in this cycle, which is the only thing that exists and shapes their life.

At times, Beckett seemed ready to be saved. He seemed to really want it. We all believed he could get there, to stay clean long enough to stop the wanting, stop the raw call for more.

*   *   *

During 2017, I was working on a new album, *The Medicine Show*, a way for me to share my passion for plant medicine through my music. I wanted to share how these naturally occurring substances—cannabis, mushrooms, psilocybin, ayahuasca—had tremendous healing properties as well as being sources of expanding consciousness and insight. In addition to celebrating these medicines through music, I began to explore how to support the legalization of them as well.

Songs like "This Human Chain" capture how we are all connected. How we need to learn to be respectful of one another, and not filled with hate or divisiveness.

> *Break my heart until it opens*
> *Move my stars across my sky*
> *Shine me up, mmm, I have seen the omens*
> *I am two spirits to the naked eye*
> *Time to come together, time to realize*

I cannot blame the other, my life is my design
Time to come together, time for me to see
My brothers and my sisters, just another part of me
Hey, uh-huh
This human chain
Will be unbroken
By and by, love, by and by
This human chain
Goes on forever
It's you and I
It's you and I
Time to come together, time to realize
I cannot blame the other, my life is my design
Time to come together, time for me to see
My brothers and my sisters, just another part of me
Time to come together, time to realize
I cannot blame the other, my life is my design
Time to come together, time for me to see
My brothers and my sisters, just another part of me
Time to come together, oh, time to realize
Time to come together
Time to come together

One of my favorite songs from that time period is "Wild and Lonely," because it has this awesome guitar solo.

Dangerous, I must confess
I hold my tongue, I hold my breath
Another night, a long dark road

With miles and miles and miles to go
A raging hollow emptiness I feel
The night is cold and I'm alone
Come and take the wheel
Because you, you've seen me in my cage
Cursed, I've been betrayed
Oh, tonight I've lost my way
And I feel so wild and lonely
Don't you wanna save me?
Don't you wanna stone me?
Hey
Oh-oh
If I could and I know I should
I'd be over this, I'd be understood
A howling moon and an ancient song
I got miles and miles to go 'til dawn
An angry craving seeps into my skin
It's all too much, I need to touch you once again
Because you, you've seen me in my cage
Cursed, I've been betrayed
Oh, tonight I've lost my way
And I feel so wild and lonely
Don't you wanna save me?
Don't you wanna stone me?
Don't you wanna save me? Oh
I feel so wild and lonely
Don't you wanna steal me?
Don't you wanna own me? (Come on)
Don't you wanna drive me?

Drive me on the highway
Don't you wanna save me?
Don't you wanna stone me?
Wild and lonely, oh
Wild and lonely
Come on, come on, save me
Don't you wanna stone me?
Wild and lonely, oh

Between the lines, I can see now that as much as I was connected to Spirit, it did nothing to keep Beckett from slipping away. I wanted desperately to help him find peace, to help him find Spirit, but I knew that I couldn't force it. He had to want to heal himself. His anger at the world was so desperate, so sad. A cry for help for sure, but a cry I didn't know how to answer except to make every resource for healing available to him. I sat in a paralyzed place of knowing that his healing was in his hands, and it was sheer torture.

I think now that *The Medicine Show* captures my struggle to be strong and truthful for myself, and brings to light the fears that lingered in the shadows. As a mom, I was living the old adage that you can only be as happy as your least happy child.

Alone with my music, I heard a truth I didn't quite want to accept. Everyone experiences pain; whether it's physical or emotional doesn't matter. Beckett's pain was too much for him. With Vicodin, he escaped the physical pain of his broken ankle and also the psychic pain of the disappointment that he would never reach his dream of being a top snowboarder. By the time he found Oxy and then heroin, it was a different pain he was trying to escape.

There's a song on *The Medicine Show* that I tucked in near the end; it's all about my worries, fears, and doubts for Beckett. I never sang it live; it was too painful to share. But when my producer, John Shanks, bless him, said to me, "Melissa, that's just too sad an ending," I added a couple of lines. I'm not sure it really took the sting out of the song.

I was bringing Beckett into my heart when I wrote that song, and I wanted to manifest that he'd be all right. The song is called "Here Comes the Pain," and it goes like this:

The bones get broken
And the skin gets torn
And the scars, they bleed
Like the day they were born
When the mouth gets wise
To the haunt's disguise
Here comes the pain
Here comes the pain
Well, the dreams get lost
In the clouds of sorrow
And the hopelessness
Is hard to swallow
Beyond repair
What the soul can bear
Here comes the pain
Here comes the pain, hey
And it feels like kissing Jesus
As it melts into your veins
When the whole damn world is busted
There's no need in bein' sane

Beyond repair
What the soul can bear
The nerves, they tear
Dying a death of despair, oh
Here comes the pain
Here comes the pain, oh
Here comes the pain
Here comes the pain
Hold on, I'm comin'
Hold on, I am comin'
Hear me
Who's gonna hear this?
Oh, oh, who's gonna feel this?
Oh, oh, who's gonna hear this?
Oh, oh, who is gonna feel this?

CHAPTER 11

LIVING IN LOCKDOWN

I was thinking recently about something my astrologer once told me years ago, long before I became a mother. Every year for my birthday, I'd seek her out to touch base with the world we cannot see but I know is there. She told me that I was going to have three children, the first one willful—and that is absolutely Bailey.

My second child, the astrologer said, would be my work. Indeed, Beckett was work—energy to get him up in the morning, energy to calm and soothe him, energy to help him discover interests and passion. Endless work.

She also said that I would have a third child who would be my soul—ah, the lovely twins, who must have appeared in her vision joined as one. Even though they are just starting out, beginning to carve their own paths, I can see that their belief in the world and what it holds for them is deeply soulful. They are not materialistic. They not about wanting things in the world. They seem to know that this world is about the experience. I wouldn't be surprised if they were working with me at the Etheridge Foundation five years from now. They look on the world as a unified whole and somehow intuit that the life of the individual self is limiting.

I also see how much the world has changed in the almost-ten years between the twins and Bailey and Beckett; there's a marked difference between the two sets of kids, with Bailey and of course Beckett feeling so much pressure—to do, to succeed, to be someone other than their true selves. I do think Bailey is figuring out how to serve the world the best she can. She wants to do meaningful work. And I know she will.

The astrologer seemed to know that Beckett was going to have trouble. As he struggled with his addiction, and as I sat on the not-remote sidelines, I sometimes saw him as not meant for this earthly existence. As a child, he was an old soul, fluid and fluent in nature, a nimble but vulnerable firefly who could never rest—showing sparks of brilliance but often finding himself in the dark.

The astrologer said that souls like his have an opportunity to make sense of themselves and the world. They have a choice to go through hard work and change the world . . . or check out and try again another time.

Even as a child I could see him try to discern this choice. He took the *everything is against me* and *the world is fucked up* attitude and leaned into it like that was going to help him or absolve him. The world *is* totally fucked up—there's no denying it. But one could say it has always been that way. But the world has also always been wondrous. We are all trying the best we can to get through and to be more of light than darkness. But sometimes, and for some, it's just too hard. For Beckett, the fact that the regular ins and outs of daily living didn't really make sense to him, his life was one drawn-out struggle.

The astrologer also predicted that his years from nineteen to twenty-one would be the hardest, telling me that if he makes it past twenty-one, he's going to be okay. This gave me hope.

Even though astrology is one of the oldest sciences, I didn't think what she was telling me was automatically Beckett's destiny. It's always up to us to create our lives.

I was not giving up hope. As a parent, that is impossible, but I think some part of me was preparing myself for loss. Is that even possible? I wonder now. To be both hopeful and despairing? Is there a place where those two forces meet and become something other, something meaningful? I'm not sure I can answer that question.

I was reminded of a song that Bailey, Beckett, and I would sometimes sing together. I think we all knew it was about and for Beckett, and we sang it as a unit. I played one of my favorite acoustic guitars, and Bailey and Beckett would sing harmony. It's called "Lost in My Mind" by a great band, the Head and the Heart; it goes like this:

Put your dreams away for now
I won't see you for some time
I am lost in my mind
I get lost in my mind
Momma once told me
"You're already home where you feel loved"
I am lost in my mind
I get lost in my mind
Oh, my brother
Your wisdom is older than me

But oh, my brother

Don't you worry about me

Don't you worry

Don't you worry, don't worry about me

Ooh, ooh, ooh, ooh

Ooh, ooh

Ooh, ooh, ooh, ooh

How's that bricklayin' comin'?

How's your engine runnin'?

Is that bridge gettin' built?

Are your hands gettin' filled?

Won't you tell me, my brother?

'Cause there are stars

Up above

And we can start

Moving forward

Ooh, ooh

Ooh, ooh, ooh, ooh

Ooh, ooh

Ooh, ooh, ooh, ooh

How's that bricklayin' comin'?

How's your engine runnin'?

Is that bridge gettin' built?

Are your hands gettin' filled?

Won't you tell me, my brother?

'Cause there are stars

Up above

We can start

Moving forward

Lost in my mind

Lost in my mind
Oh, I get lost in my mind
Lost, I get lost
I get lost in my mind
Lost in my mind
Yes, I get lost in my mind
Lost, I get lost
I get lost
Oh, I get lost
Oh, I get

The repetition of the song is what gets me. I hear his struggle. The pain that Beckett could not seem to extinguish. If only... if only.

After Christmas of 2019, Beckett did go to rehab, but as soon as he detoxed, he left the program. Again. He couldn't seem to understand that living clean was not just a matter of getting the drugs out of his system. That it meant truly changing the way he lived in his head and in his daily life.

He reached out to me to help him make a plan. He wanted to move back to Colorado and start spending more time outdoors again. It seemed like the only place he'd ever been happy. I was hopeful once again.

He found an apartment in Denver and tried to get a license to sell cannabis since Colorado had recently made it legal, and hence safer. And though I had my doubts about this direction for Beckett, I again succumbed to wanting to believe in him. I knew other people who had been addicted to drugs—even the very hard ones, like heroin—who now lived close to that old life but from a healthy, safe place.

Might this work for Beckett?

My fingers were crossed. My heart was in knots. I tried to call upon Spirit to help me believe that he had a fighting chance. I could not give up on him.

Beckett would call or text me every day. I preferred hearing his voice; I wanted to hear its timbre. If it was flat, I figured he was using. Sometimes I'd ask him to FaceTime me, so I could see him. When he looked disheveled, with a grayness to his complexion, I knew he was using. I was beginning to resign myself to the fact that he might not ever stop using.

I wrestled with what to do. I wanted desperately to believe there was a chance he could find power within to fight this demon of addiction, a power not yet eviscerated by the drugs. There were moments, though, when I would fall into a waking despair.

Hadn't we done everything possible to get Beckett help? Therapists? Education? Wilderness opportunities? Treatment centers— inpatient and outpatient? Was I missing something? Something I might still do?

His calls proclaiming his desire to get better became an empty refrain. We'd heard it so many times before, but he sounded more and more paranoid. He became obsessed with guns again and got caught up in crazy conspiracy theories fueled in part by the grotesque circus coming out of the White House at that time and some media outlets.

THE PANDEMIC

March 2020 came and the world shut down. The pandemic was our new reality. No one had a playbook for what to do or what was to come. It was harder for some than others.

Bailey had come home. She'd gone on what she expected to be a vacation to St. Barts with a close friend. They flew from New York just as COVID lockdown began, and as soon as they landed, the island warned them that they had twenty-four hours before they closed the airports. They flew back to the family's home in Washington, DC.

About a day later, when Bailey heard from the investment bank where she worked that all employees could work remotely, she decided to come home to California. I was relieved. I wanted my family together. The twins were especially thrilled that she was home.

I was grateful that I had my family around me, or most of them. We quickly became our own pod and began all sorts of rituals. We did puzzles, watched movies, and played board games. We cooked together and found great comfort being with one another.

Beckett seemed far away in Denver. He checked in with me every couple of days, and I'd update Linda and the kids. But I didn't say much; he didn't sound good.

About two weeks in, on March 16, 2020, I woke up and thought to myself, *I've got to do something to share with the world beyond our walls.* I decided to do what I do best—play some music! With Linda's help, I set up a microphone in my office and decided on a couple of songs that I then performed for my very first live-stream concert. I called it the Lockdown Concert! What a relief to feel like I was connected to the outside world. We were all trying to stay healthy—body and mind—and I wanted to extend a feeling that we were all in this together. To share some love with everyone.

Linda helped produce, and we rearranged my office into a make-shift studio. There was so much sadness all around and, like everyone else, we were all just trying to keep our wits about us. The music helped. The first song I performed was "Pulse"–it had so many layers of meaning by that time.

We got into a routine with these perform-from-home shows. I prepared all morning until about noon, and then at three p.m.–showtime!

Seventeen days later we were still going strong and learning every day. By April 1, 2020, Linda and I were into a rhythm. That day I performed "Message to Myself," "The Wanting of You," and "This Human Chain," then closed with "Sleep." I was so grateful for all the people who were lining the shelves in the stores, the delivery people, the nurses and doctors in the hospitals. I wanted to contribute in some small way and do what I knew best: make music.

I played music from all of my albums–starting with *Melissa Etheridge* and getting all the way to *One Way Out*, an album I'd been compiling since 2014, which would eventually become the tour I did in 2021–22.

We started airing the concerts using my phone and Facebook Live; then I called Ozzie, my sound man, to help me hook up a looper and set up a different camera. We were definitely figuring it out!

By day twenty-five, after dealing with a few days of Wi-Fi problems, I was playing in the dark, still in my office, trying to go live with the help of my manager. Thousands of people tuned in to watch it live or later. For me, my creative energy was gathering steam.

And then on day fifty-seven, everything in my life changed.

* * *

We had not heard much from Beckett for over a week, and we all were getting worried. It was a Sunday–I had gone to the market;

thankfully the Trader Joe's near us was fully stocked with fresh foods, lucky for us living in California. I was masked up like a zombie as I drove when Beckett FaceTimed me. I pulled over so we could talk. He was miserable. He was alone. They had closed all the parks, so he couldn't skateboard or bicycle. He couldn't go anywhere. Work was impossible in his current state.

He just kept saying over and over again, "I can't do this, I can't do this." He was moaning and groaning in bed in his apartment in Denver, his computer at the bottom of his bed for our FaceTime.

He said, "I'm sick. Mom, it's fentanyl."

Linda and I had talked about our worries that Beckett had moved from heroin to fentanyl. We knew that it was easy to get it in Denver.

I said, "I'm calling the ambulance."

He said, "No, don't do it." And he hung up.

I didn't hear from him Monday morning. I emailed Julie—email, now, the only way we could safely communicate—and told her that Beckett was not at all well. Julie emailed me back that she would call in a welfare check. The police went over and then called us back.

"He's out of it, but he said he's fine," they told us, so they left.

In these situations, parents are completely hamstrung. When the police show up, they decide if the addicted person is in immediate danger to himself or others, and they are unable to do more. If Beckett had said anything directly threatening to another person or vocalized the wish to harm himself, the police would have been able to take him to a nearby emergency room for acute psychiatric inpatient care. That didn't happen, so the police just left.

We could do nothing but wait. Beckett was the only one who could do anything to help himself.

Then it was Tuesday, and still no word from Beckett.

I was pacing, trying to distract myself with the show. But I was beyond worried, again feeling useless.

When by Wednesday morning we still hadn't heard from him, Julie sent another welfare check. I was at home, waiting to hear back and trying to keep my day as normal as possible.

I went into the shower to get ready for the show, and when I came out, I could hear Bailey crying in the next room. Linda met her at the door of our bedroom, and they came into the bathroom. Bailey was wailing, "He's dead, he's dead!"

Then I got an email from Julie: "He's dead." Then another email: "And I blame you."

Over the course of that week, when he hadn't been in touch, I'd been dreading that he might die. I was keeping these fears from Linda, just keeping my thoughts to myself. But now I thought about all the choices I didn't make. I could have gotten on a plane to try to help him myself. I could have tried to bring him home. This long list of coulds and shoulds kept running through my head like a blinking light that would not stop.

Another voice was yelling in my head, *You can't save him, Melissa. You've tried, and that is not helping him. He can only save himself. If he dies, you'll have to be able to walk through this.*

It was all so profoundly sad.

When I found out I had cancer, it was immediately broadcast because I had to cancel a bunch of shows. My manager at the time told me not to tell people I had cancer because he thought it would make me look weak. I knew better: not telling the truth is a trap.

I knew that I was about to tell the world that my son had died of an opioid overdose. Yes, there was the possibility that I would be blamed, but even considering that made me the center of the story.

And I was not. Beckett's death was the only thing at that moment. My reputation is beside the point. But what do I do with the pain? What does one do with the pain?

You stop and you breathe—you breathe deeply, because a deep breath is telling your nervous system you're okay. For the past twenty years, I'd been practicing living in a nonreactive way. I was observing and moving with my breath—in and out, in and out, and that's what I did do in those minutes and hours and days after learning of my son's death.

I used my breath as I also acknowledged every wave of guilt and shame. And as I teetered on the precipice of dissolving into that guilt and shame, I would breathe and try to be steady for my family, who were engulfed with loss and sudden grief.

When I woke up the next morning, I was still inside my dream. And in that twilight place, I looked at my phone and thought I saw a text from Beckett, saying, *No pain.*

I believed it was Beckett telling me he was out of pain, and I thought, *That's good, he is finally out of pain.* I closed my eyes and brought my son into my mind, into my heart.

I went silent. The whole house shut down.

I didn't know where to turn to process my pain, so I retreated to my garage. I thought: *Like father, like daughter.*

Filled with the detritus of a full life, the garage was overgrown with mementos from my concerts, old furniture, kids' bikes, skateboards and skis, books. Put it this way: the garage was a mess, and it felt the way I did inside.

I decided to put my energies into clearing out the space to create a new music studio. Music has been my way through the most difficult parts of my life, and I hoped that focusing on it anew would be a path toward accepting that Beckett was no longer with us. I was not able to play, much less keep up my live-stream concert, so for now, I needed to purge and build. I needed to reconnect to myself and my music in hopes that it would do something—anything—to assuage my grief.

I was on autopilot, numb to the new reality that Beckett was no longer a living being, but I thought that maybe if I created a new space for my music, a safe place where I could be alone, I could process my grief.

Linda and Bailey were in tatters. Their agony and despair audible and palpable. My younger two children, the thirteen-year-old twins, Johnnie Rose and Miller, were struggling to grasp that their older brother was never coming home again. Everyone was a mess, and when I was inside the house with the rest of my family, I fell into my old pattern of trying to be the strong one, the one holding and hugging. Feeding and providing relief. I did as much as I could, but I needed the aloneness to feel all of what was inside of me.

At times, Linda and Bailey would come into the garage and help put the studio together. Mostly, I wanted solitude to clean, purge, rearrange, build. I turn to using my hands when I need to find solace or to problem-solve, though I knew there was no problem-solving to be done.

All my motion in those days right after Beckett passed was directed at getting back to my music. It was as if I were digging through a pile of debris to find a relic to remind me I had the strength to move forward, to move through this pain and get to the other side—the other side of what, I did not know.

I couldn't play yet, couldn't sing. I was afraid of how I'd sound. My voice might crack; I might break down into tears. Singing until then had always saved me, but this was different. This was a pain so deep that I was afraid if I opened my heart—the only way I know how to sing—I might collapse under the weight of the grief that lived there and never recover. So I cleaned and purged and re-arranged instead.

Building my new studio was one of the first steps in my healing journey.

The next step was when I decided to reconnect to my people, the audience I'd been playing for since the lockdown had started in March. About a month had passed since Beckett had died, and with the help and encouragement of Linda and Bailey, I put together a live-stream concert I called the Heal M.E. Concert.

I needed to sing and to share and to connect with my audience, to ask them for help healing from the most brutal loss of my life. I'd never asked anything of them before, though I'd certainly received plenty. But this was a direct plea for help.

Performing is a two-way street: I give love and receive love. In the days and weeks following Beckett's death, I needed all the love—coming and going—I could get.

I planned a few songs and then went live. I didn't want to re-hearse, because in performing I was trying to live in the moment of what it meant to share myself in this way—my way, through singing and playing guitar—a vital act of catharsis.

On the edge of tears, I opened the concert by talking about Beck-ett, how we as a family had received an outpouring of love over the past month—the love had flowed through all the flowers, the food baskets, the notes, the texts, and the emails. I wanted people to know we were okay and we were beyond grateful.

Then, my voice almost breaking, I sang "You Are My Sunshine"—

that old lullaby, performed in so many ways, a song I sang to my own kids as they were growing up and still do. I closed my eyes and sang to my sweet boy. I could feel him in and around me as I sang the simple lyrics.

You are my sunshine, my only sunshine

Tears filled my eyes as I sang. Singing such a private song in public may have felt awkward if I had not been in the garage that I had so carefully transformed into an intimate space for me and my music. I closed my eyes and let the song flow out of me.

I then moved into a song I had written way back in the '90s– "Talking to My Angel." Sung now as a kind of plea mixed with a promise:

> *Don't be afraid*
> *Close your eyes*
> *Lay it all down*
> *Don't you cry*
> *Can't you see I'm going*
> *Where I can see the sun rise*
> *I've been talking to my angel*
> *And he said that it's all right*

The song had taken on new meaning, like many songs do for me over the years. I'd written this one after my dad died. I was thirty years old then, and thought of myself as a hard-charging woman striving for fame and making real my dream of becoming a rock star. My father, my first and biggest champion, was no longer a phone call away, but I talked to him anyway. He is one of my angels.

On that late afternoon in my newly transformed garage studio,

I was doing all I could to sing for Beckett. I envisioned him: I saw that he'd stopped running, he'd found peace, he'd found freedom. I wanted him to know—I was trying to tell him—that we were all going to be all right. And I wanted desperately for that to be true.

Next, I sang "Here Comes the Pain," a song I'd written about Beckett when he was in the throes of his disease. I'd never sung it in concert before that day, and making the pain public felt somehow essential. Necessary.

Hold on, I'm comin'
Hold on, I am comin'
Hear me
Who's gonna hear this?
Oh, oh, who's gonna feel this?
Oh, oh, who's gonna hear this?
Oh, oh, who is gonna feel this?

I then asked my dear sweet daughter Bailey to join me for a song we'd often sung together over the years.

When Bailey was twelve, I was working on a song about her growing up, how she was on that slippery razor's edge between being a child and becoming a young woman. I wanted to express how scary it felt for me as a mother to know that I would eventually have to let her go. But let go we mothers must. This precious angel of mine, so close, was going to leave my side eventually, but always return.

I was working out the lyrics and the music on my guitar, when I noticed that Bailey had snuck into the room. She'd been sitting quiet as a mouse, listening. Then she popped up and said, "Mama, I think you should add the word 'together' to the last refrain."

Now, most people don't make suggestions about my music, but my brave Bailey could, and I smiled as she ventured close to me.

The song was on my *Fearless Love* album, and it was called "Gently We Row," and it goes like this:

When my soul crashed into my body
Falling into consciousness
That's when my mind began this illusion
Of taking it step after step
I looked into mother's eyes
I said tell me what I should believe
She drew me a room with a light and said
Just turn it off when you leave
Slow, slow, this river is slow
We're all out here on our own
Row, row, gently we row
One day we'll find our way home
Step after step
They drew me a town
They drew me a fear and a need
They drew me a god and
They drew me some money
Hiding the truth far from me
I asked the cool fire light
Tell me, what I should believe
And they gave me a song
And they gave me a dance
And said sleep now, your pain will relieve
Slow, slow, this river is slow

And we're all out here on our own

Row, row, gently we row

And one day we'll find our way home

I've stumbled and crawled

I've begged to know why

And I've been ashamed

When I've chosen to lie

In all of this darkness

I have searched for a light

To come and find me

And when I found me

I wrapped my arms round

My own daughter as she fell into her place and time

And as her mind creates her illusions

I won't complicate hers with mine

She looked into her mother's eyes

She said tell me what I should believe

And I drew her a door

And I drew her a key

And I said when you're ready you'll come and find me

And we'll walk out of here and tomorrow will be a new day

Slow, slow, this river is slow

And you are never out here on your own

Row, row, gently we row

Oh

*And **together** we'll find our way*

Slow, slow, this river is slow

Life is not what it seems

Row, row, gently we row

The truth is
It's only a dream

Whenever I've sung this song in concert and come to the line, "I won't complicate hers with mine," the mothers in the audience cry out—in satisfying recognition. Mothering can be so hard.

But Bailey was right: we have found our way, together. And we were healing in real time.

MAY 2021

The family is all in the backyard, the craggy lawn spilling back toward Beckett's old skateboard ramp. The Santa Monica mountains grace the backdrop. The scent of sage, lavender, and rosemary sweeten the air. I am home in this place.

We are assembled before the wooden bench a fan made for me, and I hold a velvet bag of ashes in my hand and look out to my loves—Linda, Bailey, Johnnie Rose, and Miller. It's been a year since Beckett passed from this world. Although we can thank COVID for postponing any service, the truth is that none of us had been near ready to formally say good-bye to Beckett. And I'll speak for myself: I wasn't sure if I could withstand the pain.

Earlier that day, I had found a hawk's feather that had fallen from the sky. I held it now, feeling Beckett's presence.

In my mind's eye, I see the little boy running toward the ocean, I feel his sweaty hand in mine, I smell his hair. These emotional memories are clear and visceral.

The quiet simplicity of the family gathering is fitting, and I am sure that Beckett would approve. Beckett loved the outdoors, and in a big, cacophonous world that he often found difficult to navigate, we were his people.

I burn some white sage and wave it toward the mountains and into the hot, dry wind.

I say a few words, telling him, "Buddy, I get it. I know that life was too hard for you here. I understand that you just couldn't make it in this life."

I knew he would agree that it was ridiculous for me to torture myself. He'd seen me tortured long enough.

Then I dig my hand into the velvet bag and pull out a fistful. Tears run down my face, and I let the ashes fly.

I will miss my boy, my beautiful son. But I keep his light within me; its warmth and gentle nudge are a part of me, now and forever.

AFTERWORD

"I went to the woods because I wished to live deliberately, to front only the essential facts of life, and see if I could not learn what it had to teach, and not, when I came to die, discover that I had not lived. I did not wish to live what was not life, living is so dear; nor did I wish to practise resignation, unless it was quite necessary. I wanted to live deep and suck out all the marrow of life, to live so sturdily and Spartan-like as to put to rout all that was not life, to cut a broad swath and shave close, to drive life into a corner, and reduce it to its lowest terms . . ."

HENRY DAVID THOREAU

I miss him every day. I can accept that he's in a nonphysical place now, but I can reach him, just like I can reach my dad. The pain is still transforming in real time. I remind myself to return to my breath, knowing just how incredibly important it is for me to stay centered, open to all the thoughts and feelings washing through me. I can no longer hide from contradictions or messiness. I try and stay still in my knowledge of Spirit, aware that I'm going to let the others close to me in my life have their pain. I don't want to interfere. I don't want to step in and try to control or do anything more than love them with all I've got.

On the night Beckett died, we all came together—me and Linda, Bailey, Miller and Johnnie Rose, and even Julie's ex-husband, who's now a close friend, and his daughter Glynnis, whom he had with Julie. Bailey and Glynnis are close, and I think they needed each other and to share their tie to Beckett. Since it was COVID, we were still in lockdown. We got through the day and ate our favorite foods and cried together all day.

Beckett has been the ultimate challenge to me accepting the middle ground between love and fear, joy and suffering. While I can accept that he has passed from this earthly life, I will never accept that he had to die—no mother can.

Beckett's death required that I surrender to the suffering that living with Spirit sometimes entails, and I've come to realize that if I was able to not break under the loss of him, that I will be okay. My love for Beckett has not changed, nor has it disappeared. That love is both the source of the joy I feel when I am in his spirit presence, and the pain I feel when I miss his physical presence. But it is love, pure and simple. Living in Spirit means being able to access and accept that love and what it brings, no matter what it brings. Learning to surrender to it: that's where joy lives. Who says love is easy? Love can be hard, though yes, it is sometimes easy. No matter. It remains love.

My being alive does not make Beckett less dead. But my being alive does mean that I can continue to live and to show up for those I love. For my music. It's a testament to Spirit, the source of wonder and awe that is always there for us if we open our hearts to it. I don't need to remind myself that alongside wonder and awe are loss and sorrow. Beckett taught me that hard lesson. But through it all is love. Only love.

ALIVE

Sometimes the shortest distance is the longest road.

Sometimes the highest price that's paid is that which is not owed.

Sometimes the strongest soldier is the one who yields his sword.

Sometimes the sweet surrender comes from a single word.

I am alive, I have survived, and I'm holding on.

I am alive, and I'm moving on.

I'm moving on.

I'm moving on.

Sometimes the brightest hope comes from the darkest night.

Sometimes the broken dream can set your wings to flight.

Sometimes you take a trip through hell to see heaven above and shake hands with the devil to find an angel's love.

I am alive, I have survived, and I'm holding on.

I am alive, and I'm moving on.

I'm moving on.

I am alive.

Sometimes the sweetest answer is just beneath your skin and all the world is waiting for you to let it in.

I am alive.

Oh, I have survived and I'm holding on.

I am alive.

I have survived, and I'm holding on.

I am alive, and I'm moving on.

I'm moving on.

ACKNOWLEDGMENTS

A lot of creative work is collaborative, and many of those close to me helped bring this book alive. I would like to extend my deep appreciation to my editor at Harper Wave, Karen Rinaldi, who believed in this project from the beginning. I'd also like to thank my manager and the woman who makes it all happen, Deb Klein; my literary agent, Yfat Reiss Gendell; and my cowriter, Billie Fitzpatrick, whose brilliant work helped shape and create this book.

Big thanks and love go out to my family—Linda, Bailey, Miller Steven, and Johnnie Rose—you are all my heart and my soul.

And a huge thanks to Steven Girmant, my friend, who has been by my side for so much of my life.

ME

PERMISSIONS

Lost in My Mind
Words and Music by CHRIS ZASCHE, JOSIAH JOHNSON, CHARITY ROSE THIELEN, KENNY HENSLEY, TYLER WILLIAMS and JONATHAN RUSSELL
© 2011 BUDDIES AND SNACKS and SNACKS AND BUDDIES
All Rights for BUDDIES AND SNACKS Administered by WC MUSIC CORP.
All Rights for SNACKS AND BUDDIES Administered by WARNER-TAMERLANE PUBLISHING CORP.
All Rights Reserved
Used by Permission of ALFRED MUSIC

A Little Bit of Me
Words and Music by Melissa Etheridge, Jon Levine, Jerrod Michael Bettis and Christian Seibert
Copyright © 2014 1902 Miami, Sony Music Publishing Canada, Old Schul Music Inc., WC Music Corp., Margetts Road Music, Asternaut and Christian Seibert Publishing Designee
All Rights for 1902 Miami Administered by BMG Rights Management (US) LLC
All Rights for Sony Music Publishing Canada and Old Schul Music, Inc. Administered by Sony Music Publishing (US) LLC, 424 Church Street, Suite 1200, Nashville, TN 37219
All Rights for WC Music Corp., Margetts Road Music and Asternaut Administered by WC Music Corp.
Reprinted by Permission of Hal Leonard LLC

Alive
Words and Music by Melissa Etheridge
Copyright © 2002 Songs Of Ridge Road
All Rights Administered by BMG Rights Management (US) LLC
All Rights Reserved Used by Permission
Reprinted by Permission of Hal Leonard LLC

California
Words and Music by Melissa Etheridge

Copyright © 2007 Songs Of Ridge Road
All Rights Administered by BMG Rights Management (US) LLC
All Rights Reserved Used by Permission
Reprinted by Permission of Hal Leonard LLC

Company
Words and Music by Melissa Etheridge
Copyright © 2010 Songs Of Ridge Road
All Rights Administered by BMG Rights Management (US) LLC
All Rights Reserved Used by Permission
Reprinted by Permission of Hal Leonard LLC

Down To One
Words and Music by Melissa Etheridge
Copyright © 2001 MLE Music
All Rights Administered by BMG Rights Management (US) LLC
All Rights Reserved Used by Permission
Reprinted by Permission of Hal Leonard LLC

Gently We Row
Words and Music by Melissa Etheridge
Copyright © 2010 Songs Of Ridge Road
All Rights Administered by BMG Rights Management (US) LLC
All Rights Reserved Used by Permission
Reprinted by Permission of Hal Leonard LLC

Here Comes the Pain
Words and Music by Melissa Etheridge
Copyright © 2019 1902 Miami
All Rights Administered by BMG Rights Management (US) LLC
All Rights Reserved Used by Permission
Reprinted by Permission of Hal Leonard LLC

I Need to Wake Up
Words and Music by Melissa Etheridge
Copyright © 2005 Songs Of Ridge Road
All Rights Administered by BMG Rights Management (US) LLC
All Rights Reserved Used by Permission
Reprinted by Permission of Hal Leonard LLC

SEP 2023